WRINKLIES™
Puzzle Book

Published in 2018 by Prion
An imprint of the Carlton Publishing Group
20 Mortimer Street
London W1T 3JW

Layout and design copyright © 2018 Carlton Books Limited
Wrinklies is a trademark of Carlton Books Ltd

A CIP catalogue record of this book can be obtained from the British Library

ISBN 978 1 91161 009 0

Printed in Dubai

10 9 8 7 6 5 4 3 2 1

The puzzles in this book previously appeared in *Brain Training Puzzles: Quick Book 1, Quick Book 2, Intermediate Book 1, Intermediate Book 2, Difficult Book 1, Difficult Book 2, House of Puzzles Holiday Puzzles, House of Puzzles Travel Puzzles, House of Puzzles Sudoku, Lateral Thinking Puzzles, Lateral Thinking Posers, Wrinklies' Travel Puzzles*

WRINKLIES™
Puzzle Book

Clever Conundrums for Older Intellects

PRION

Contents

Introduction

The key to staying youthful is keeping the mind active. In your senior years you (hopefully) have more time to devote to hobbies and pastimes, and there is no better way to pass the time than giving your grey matter a workout.

Puzzles are particularly useful in sharpening your perception, memory, logic and reasoning – all of which can become casualties in your autumn years if you chose to stimulate your brain with nothing more thought provoking than the TV guide.

The conundrums in this book have been specially chosen with the Wrinkly puzzle-lover in mind. We hope you enjoy this collection and remember that where the mind goes, the heart will follow. Here's to many more years of youth.

EASY
PUZZLES

Word search

```
S U R U Z H K S I R U O O N P
L U H O F C T H U L H U N K E
A N E I G L R N Y K U R O S T
T R R D N U O L N E R E I O O
N E E S O M E E I M P L R T H
E I S P E M Y G L T R A A A T
M F S D R U S B B L V B G T A
E S I A N A J A O P E K I A L
L C N M F A U N G D I B A R R
E U S P A M M R B W B F A E A
R H Y D R A E Y O O R C C D Y
E T O R U M N I H K E D V E N
T A E R I S U E B M E B M G T
A B I A S D N A S R O G A I G
W A N E E U Q R L L I H P W Z
```

ABATH	GREMIAN	NUN
AGAPE	HILL	NYARLATHOTEP
APSU	HOBBIT	NYKUR
ARION	HOBGOBLIN	ORC
ASMODEUS	HU	PIT
BEL	HYDRA	QUEEN
BIASDNASROGAIG	ICE	RABID
CTHULHU	IMP	RATATOSK
ECIDEMON	ISA	ROGUE
ERIS	LEGBA	URISK
FAUN	MAD	URUS
FIRE	MBEMBE	WABE
GEDE	NISSE	WATERELEMENTAL

Sudoku

8	6							3
							9	
9		2	4		3			
7					5	4		
1		3						
		6				8		
		5	7	4		3		
								9
3				1	8	7		2

The X-ray film

Robert Blocker, approaching his fortieth birthday, had never been abroad. He enjoyed his vacations in Torquay and being in charge of UK marketing, he never had a need to travel. All this was to change when he was promoted to the position of export manager for the South American market. He was delighted with the opportunity to visit all these exotic countries. Strangely, though, on every trip he took with him an x-ray film made about 10 years before.

Considering that Blocker was in perfect health and had no intention of consulting a doctor, and his company was in the textile business, how do you account for this unusual habit?

Maze

Spot the difference

Can you spot ten differences between this pair of pictures?

Shape shifting

Fill in the empty squares so that each row, column and long diagonal contains six different symbols

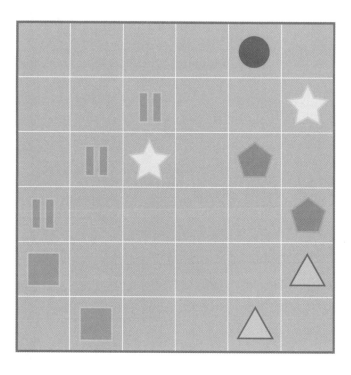

Word search

```
K S T E W N C G E C I U J C L
D E G E O N M U J P S L U T I
I G B N M C A H P A C R P U I
S C G A N I H E L F R L F C K
H I X O B T L A S Y U S L K Q
M E V O L C D G R G B L A E V
V E H G I B P O K M B A N R U
N M U F A F F B E K I V K Y A
U R V R D R A L U K N I S E I
M A I N E R T E E A G A B Y R
F S O A P S G T G R B N S P G
T E A C L C U V G L R L B U N
K M U G O C O F E N U A E B A
C W A I E A E R N I S M G M S
J T U M A R T I N I H J Z A Y
```

BAKER	FLANK	OVEN
BEAUNE	GOBLET	PLUG
BUN	HAM	SABLE
CAN	INFUSER	SAGE
CHAR	JUICE	SALAD BAR
CLOVE	KEBAB	SALT BOX
COAT	LARD	SANGRIA
CORN	LIME	SCRUBBING BRUSH
CUPFUL	MARTINI	SINK
CURRY	MELBA	SOAP
DISH	MELTS	STWE
ECLAIR	MIGNON	TUCKER
EGGS	MUG	VEAL

Sudoku

	3							7
			3	2				8
4							5	
	2		4				1	
3	8			5	2			
	5		1				9	
5							7	
			6	8				1
	9							4

Magic squares

Complete the square using nine consecutive numbers, so that all rows, columns and large diagonals add up to the same total.

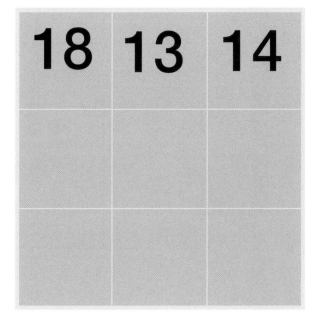

Spot the difference

Can you spot ten differences between this pair of pictures?

7		3		9			5	
6	9			2	4			1
1					5		4	
		4					6	
			2	1	6			
	6					1		
	2		8					5
9			6	4			3	8
	7			5		2		6

Word search

```
M D I V E R G E L D T J C E I
U E L L I P S O I D Q O L X R
S Q S I E D I V I D M U E N A
C U E V I T I S O P R D A C L
L J C A B S T Z L C N H R Z A
A F T H O R O E S I G N B S C
S E I R E S X N M B Q W E I S
S N O V Z N R O X U V T G M I
R A N Q U A R T I C T O L R N
A I W M T P K O C H L E A A N
D D B I I Y R N E I E E E E T
D E O V E C T O R J N M P O U
R M Z E R O R M P I A O O Q V
S I X A L Y J V L I L R C D O
I M C C U B E L O P P R I M E
```

ADD	INVERT	QED
ALGEBRA	LINEAR	QUARTIC
AXIS	LOGIC	RATIO
CLASS	MEAN	ROOT
COMPLEX NUMBER	MEDIAN	RULE
CONIC	MODE	SCALAR
CUBE	MONOTONE	SECTION
CUBIC	OPEN	SERIES
DIVERGE	PI	SET THEORY
DIVIDE	PLANE	SIGN
DIVISOR	POLE	SUM
ELLIPSOID	POSITIVE	VECTOR
INDEX	PRIME	ZERO

Spot the difference

Can you spot ten differences between this pair of pictures?

Maze

```
N X B L E Z A E T P H O S Y Z
R L O R W C G A G E J Z D A Y
O A T E O E O R A N I L H O O
C P K I A O V W S K I T H S V
J A M E D J M O U I L L I S R
T N P T X E S R L A R E P E A
E D D O E S J T C C R I I R O
N U B B I N F O A M N C P C X
B Y R D B R I A R K X A I K H
A M E N I M A D R A C N Z C I
R A I S S A C O L O I E N O P
C B Z N Q N O F C I L U Z D J
T R X C T T Y A E V R E H U P
P A N I C V G D J V A N T O K
D Z A H I C S U M F G E U E P
```

ANIL	EAR-WORT	NEP
BRIAR	EDDOES	NUBBIN
BROOM	FLAX	OAT
CALTHA	GARLIC	OSIER
CANE	HERVEA	OXHIP
CARDAMINE	HOP	PANIC
CASSIA	IRIS	PEA
CLOVE	IVY	PINK ROOT
COCA	JUTE	PIPI
CORN	LING	RUE
CRAB	MINT	RUNCH
DISS	MUSCI	TEAZEL
DOCKCRESS	NAPAL	WOAD

Sudoku

	5							9
			5				3	
	2	9		8	6			
1	4	3	8			9		7
					4	5		3
7	8	5	2			1		4
	1	6		4	2			
			1				9	
	7							5

Can you spot ten differences between this pair of pictures?

Riddle

Copacabana

Gambling can be as addictive as alcohol or drugs, and Gert
Waterman had had his fair share of it. Joining Gamblers
Anonymous did the trick and he considered himself cured. His
parents were overjoyed, and as a reward gave him a Rolex and
offered to pay for a two week vacation in Rio de Janeiro.

Gert had always wanted to visit Brazil, and the thought of
escaping the gloom of a London winter for the sunny beaches of
Copacabana filled him with excited anticipation. Unfortunately he
had got into bad company during his gambling days and was left
in no doubt as to the consequences if he failed to pay the £2,500 he
still owed. He could not ask his parents after all they had done for
him, and in his desperation he sold the Rolex. Anyway, who needed
a watch when there were clocks everywhere? To Gert time was not
of the essence anyway. The proceeds just covered his debt.

Arriving in Rio he checked in at the Ouro Verde and spent the
days basking in the glorious sunshine of the Copacabana and
Ipanema beaches. The one thought which marred his otherwise
blissful happiness was how to explain the missing Rolex to his
parents.

On the last day of his vacation, fate intervened. He was on the
way to his hotel to start packing when he was mugged by a man
wielding a knife. Without hesitation, he handed over his money,
traveller's cheques and camera and, with some regret, even his
signet ring. Although there were many people around, nobody
came to his aid and the culprit at once made off with his haul.

On the way to the police station Gert suddenly had an inspiration.
This incident could be the deus ex machina of all his problems.
Police Inspector Nivaldo Garcia typed the report with the list of
items, to which Gert added the Rolex watch. He then asked for
a copy to support his insurance claim. Nivaldo hesitated for a
moment and, looking sternly at Gert, deleted the Rolex from the
list of items!

What made the Inspector take this action?

Sudoku

	5		4			7	3	
7				2		8		1
						4	9	
	8		3				5	
	7				8	1		
	9		7				2	
						9	8	
2				9		5		3
	3		8			2	1	

Spot the difference

Can you spot ten differences between this pair of pictures?

Sudoku

			8	9	6			
7		1		4		6		8
				5				
5			4	3	9			1
			1		7			
	4		2	8	5		6	
	6	9				1	3	
8				2				4
	3						5	

```
S  R  E  W  O  P  D  D  I  U  L  F  R  K  C
N  E  N  T  H  A  L  P  Y  E  D  E  F  E  A
E  C  H  A  R  M  Y  B  N  B  S  S  L  C  B
L  I  T  U  U  L  I  N  E  A  R  B  U  R  S
O  M  W  O  S  H  A  Q  M  S  M  V  X  O  O
H  A  N  N  G  H  Y  M  F  E  V  A  W  F  R
M  N  N  A  C  P  G  O  S  T  M  E  O  P  P
S  Y  S  O  I  T  R  N  O  S  O  B  R  H  T
L  D  W  D  I  X  E  O  O  O  F  P  K  I  I
A  T  E  F  J  P  N  I  C  R  F  B  B  M  V
W  R  X  W  N  V  E  Q  H  L  T  R  P  K  I
M  E  T  R  I  C  F  L  A  V  O  U  R  L  T
B  E  A  U  T  Y  L  V  R  J  L  A  E  P  Y
D  B  P  R  O  T  O  N  G  S  U  D  H  N  N
P  O  J  V  A  R  K  X  E  Q  P  E  I  C  E
```

ABSORPTIVITY	FLAVOUR	MUON
BARN	FLUID	NEUTRON
BASE	FLUX	OHM'S LAW
BEAUTY	FORCE	ORBIT
BOSON	GAS	PION
CHARGE	IMPULSE	POWER
CHARM	JFET	PROTON
DIP	LED	QUARK
DYNAMIC	LENS	TAUON
ENERGY	LINEAR	TOP
ENSEMBLE	MASER	TWO-CHANNEL
ENTHALPY	METRIC	WAVE
FLAVOR	MONO	WORK

2					3			
		8	1			7	4	
	6		4				9	8
	8	5						
				8	9			
1				4	2			9
	7					9		
	4	9						1
		3			4		5	7

Spot the difference

Can you spot ten differences between this pair of pictures?

Arrow

Complete the grid by drawing an arrow in each box that points in any one of the eight compass directions (N, E, S, W, NE, NW, SE, SW). The numbers in the outside boxes in the finished puzzle will reflect the number of arrows pointing in their direction.

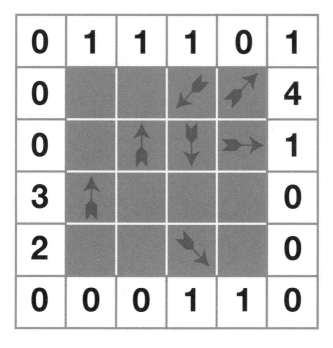

Word search

```
H  E  L  S  I  N  K  I  E  M  B  L  E  M  F
E  A  U  L  R  X  Y  Y  E  N  D  Y  S  D  L
N  R  O  S  I  L  V  E  R  E  O  H  Z  C  A
D  N  E  E  R  G  M  E  C  W  R  C  L  D  M
R  A  S  E  E  O  M  O  C  A  I  R  L  I  E
I  U  M  Z  R  R  U  U  O  L  N  O  B  D  P
A  D  S  N  I  B  R  V  N  D  G  T  L  O  F
T  C  U  O  E  P  K  E  T  I  S  T  A  N  O
R  I  I  R  L  A  G  G  I  J  C  T  C  Y  R
I  T  T  B  E  R  L  I  N  P  H  H  K  S  T
S  I  L  G  E  I  F  A  E  E  H  O  D  U  I
N  U  A  E  A  S  Y  H  N  K  T  A  U  E  U
E  S  C  E  G  L  T  S  T  Y  I  W  K  Z  S
G  E  D  E  R  S  F  I  S  L  O  N  D  O  N
U  N  E  E  T  T  I  M  M  O  C  N  Z  G  N
```

ALTIUS	FLAG	NIKE
ARNAUD	FLAME	PARIS
ATHENS	FORTIUS	PIERRE
BERLIN	GOLD	RED
BLACK	GREECE	RINGS
BLUE	GREEN	ROME
BRONZE	HAKON	SEOUL
CITIUS	HELSINKI	SILVER
COMMITTEE	HENDRIATRIS	SYDNEY
CONTINENTS	LONDON	TOKYO
DECOUBERTIN	MERLY	TORCH
DIDON	MISHA	WALDI
EMBLEM	MUNICH	ZEUS

Only two of these pictures are exactly the same. Can you spot the matching pair?

Spot the difference

Can you spot ten differences between this pair of pictures?

Only two of these pictures are exactly the same. Can you spot the matching pair?

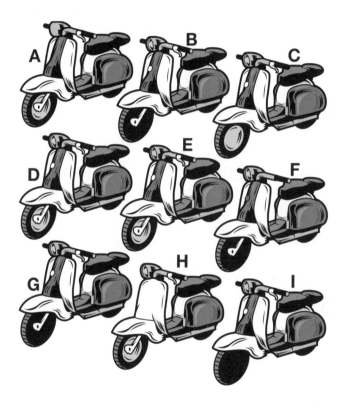

Word search

```
A L R E W U X C T H E M E D F
C I N S M E P U I O P D L O O
S M U A O T A J T T N H A R N
T I M B D I S K O F S E O E C
A T B S E N T T O F S I W N H
T I E U R I U P R U T T R N E
I N R L N F A O M T R Y E O P
V G A E M A E P S U O L V M A
E T E C T A C T H R N R I I S
E N T R T R I C N E G A T N S
S A A E U I O N E E R E A A I
U N M N B N V F W P S E D L V
A O I D P E D E L U T E S Y E
L S N U F D F P R E T E R I T
C J A S E L D D I M X B D P S
```

ACTIVE	LIMITING	RETROFLEX
ANIMATE	MAIN	ROOT
AORISTIC	MIDDLE	SONANT
APHERESIS	MODERN	SOUND
BASE	NEW	STATIVE
CLAUSE	NOMINAL	STEM
DATIVE	NUMBER	STRONG
EARLY	OLD	SURD
FINITE	PASSIVE	THEME
FUTURE	PAST	TONE
GERUND	PHONE	UNACCEPTED
HEAD	PRESENT	VOICE
LATE	PRETERIT	WEAK

Riddle

Sisters

Jane and Jessica are sitting on a park bench, two very pretty dark-haired girls as alike as two peas in a pod. A stranger walked by, looked at the girls and said, "You must be twins." The girls smiled, and Jane volunteered: "We have the same parents and were born on the same day in the same year, but we are not twins." Explain.

Sudoku

				2	1	4		5
	7		6	5		9	2	
			8					
	9	4		1			6	
		6		7		8		
	8			3		7	9	
				9				
	5	2		4	8		7	
4		8	3	6				

Spot the difference

Can you spot ten differences between this pair of pictures?

Flutter the fairy has a magic wand and wings, but she doesn't wear a crown and hasn't got a bow on her dress. Can you pick her out?

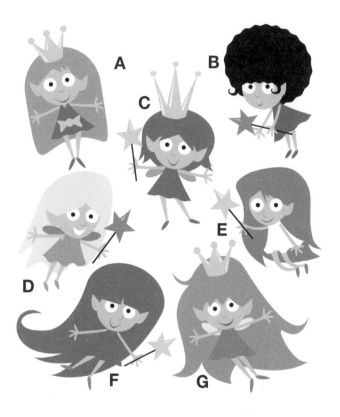

Spot the difference

Can you spot ten differences between this pair of pictures?

Riddle

A truck has stopped before a low bridge. The driver is beside himself because the bridge is exactly one inch lower than his truck is high, and this is the only route he can take to his delivery destination.

What brilliant plan do you come up with?

	8	4			9		3	
6					4			1
7		9	6			8		
		6					5	
				3			8	9
3	5			2				
		8					9	
9			8	5		7		3
	7			9			4	

Guinness or stout?

Two strangers enter a pub. The publican asks them what they would like. First man says, "I'll have a bottle of stout," and puts £2 down on the counter. Publican: "Guinness at £2 or Jubilee at £1.50?" First man: "Jubilee." Second man says, "I'll have a bottle of stout," and puts £2 on the counter. Without asking him, the publican gives him Guinness. The second man is not a regular customer, nor did he give any indication as to what he wanted.

How therefore did the publican know?

Word search

```
T  T  H  E  D  G  E  H  Y  S  S  O  P  O  A
C  M  C  L  C  L  A  R  Y  B  O  R  A  G  E
U  A  D  A  M  C  I  L  E  S  O  R  R  E  L
M  R  O  V  Z  S  A  V  A  D  N  I  B  I  H
I  J  O  E  E  E  I  M  M  N  M  A  S  A  K
N  O  W  N  V  D  L  O  O  O  G  A  T  S  Y
L  R  N  D  N  I  M  P  N  M  B  A  I  S  E
I  A  R  E  B  T  H  Y  M  E  I  S  L  A  C
T  M  E  R  U  E  E  C  P  I  B  L  X  R  U
N  Z  H  U  P  G  A  A  N  I  S  E  E  G  T
E  Q  T  P  A  P  R  I  K  A  X  P  E  E  T
M  D  U  V  E  S  S  E  R  C  I  M  N  T  E
R  I  O  R  L  D  A  O  W  N  T  N  N  G  L
O  L  S  E  S  A  M  E  U  U  E  I  A  P  R
T  L  Y  B  A  L  M  J  N  B  M  S  O  H  K
```

AGRIMONY	DILL	PAPRIKA
ANISE	ENDIVE	PARSLEY
BALM	GALANGAL	RUE
BASIL	GRASS	SAGE
BAY	HEDGE HYSSOP	SENNA
BENNET	JUNIPER	SESAME
BORAGE	LAVENDER	SIMPLE
CAMOMILE	LETTUCE	SORREL
CAPERS	LOVAGE	SOUTHERNWOOD
CHIVE	MACE	TANSY
CLARY	MARJORAM	THYME
CRESS	MINT	TORMENTIL
CUMIN	NUTMEG	WOAD

Signpost

Can you crack the logical secret behind the distances to these great cities, and work out how far it is to Mumbai?

Can you spot ten differences between this pair of pictures?

Jigsaw

Which three of the pieces below can complete the jigsaw and make a perfect square?

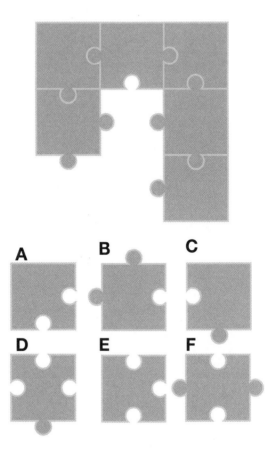

	3	2				9	4	
			3	4	6			
			1	9	5			
4	5			3			9	7
	6			7			1	
	4	6		8		2	3	
2								8
7								9

The operation

A man went to the hospital with a suspected malignant tumour in his left kidney. Several tests were made but the results were all negative. Nevertheless, the man insisted on an operation to remove the kidney. Why?

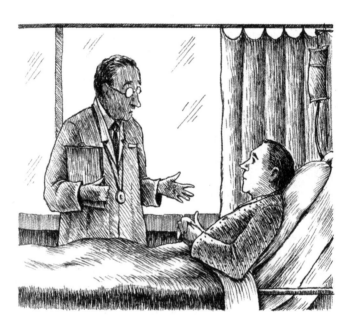

```
H X G I E K C E O G E N T G A
M C B T O R A N G E F O B W U
C R A B A P P L E A O L I V E
O D R E N N E T F I G L T X L
X K B T P I G N U T Q E T Q K
D H A P R Z A E W E P R E U N
W E D K S U A A L P A O R E U
H P O P I A H P A O P M A E T
O Y S K E G R W O X I R L N K
R D C E P C P R J T N G M I Z
T U H G M A A I X O E R O N R
W R E R W I Z N T M G O N G H
J I R I P A L T T R B U D G K
V A R O I V R U S S E T U B K
J N Y T H U N G C O L M A R S
```

ARNOT	GROUT	PECAN
BARBADOS CHERRY	HAW	PIGNUT
BITTER ALMOND	HEP	QUEENING
COLMAR	HIP	RASP
COX	KAKI	RENNET
CRAB-APPLE	LIME	RUSSET
DATE	MORELLO	SKEG
DURIAN	NUTMEG	TANGELO
EGRIOT	OGEN	UGH
ELK NUT	OLIVE	UVA
FIG	ORANGE	WHORT
GAGE	PAWPAW	WHURT
GENIPAP	PEACH	ZAPOTE

Spot the difference

Can you spot ten differences between this pair of pictures?

Sudoku

	5						8	
7		4	9	8	2	1		6
8								2
	4		6		9		3	
3				2				1
		9				5		
			7	9	8			
		7	5		3	2		
9								8

Spot the difference

Can you spot ten differences between this pair of pictures?

```
A B O U T L A S T N I G H T M
R A A F H A M A D E U S W A S
A C Y T A O B A S O C A S R T
I L I B M R O X G C S H A H B
L L L F B A G K O L B C E C N
R E X A F O N O H A O M O O Z
A H B N S A B D D K E O S K D
I E W O T O R B L X Y A C E E
L D B O I A O T I A E I T E T
Y O R T R Y I C W S L P S R B
C C L A S S A A N C E Z O A U
R H H L I N T E H C T I H Y B
A A E P B S P J C V G I G L I
S T R A A O G A V I H Z R D G
H D O C T G M R I F E H T S W
```

ABOUT LAST NIGHT	CLICK	MASH
ACCEPTED	CRASH	OPEN SEASON
AMADEUS	DR. ZHIVAGO	PLATOON
BABEL	E.T.	RAY
BAD BOYS	FARGO	SAHARA
BASOC	GHOST	SAW
BATMAN	GIGLI	TANK
BE COOL	HEAT	THE FIRM
BIG	HELLCAB	THE MEXICAN
BOBBY	HERO	TRAFFIC
CARS	HITCH	TROY
CASTAWAY	HOOK	WILD HOGS
CLASS	LIAR, LIAR	ZOOM

Wolf among the sheep

An old wolf had spent days crossing a vast wasteland without anything to eat. Starving, he came upon a large metal enclosure in the middle of a field. Inside the compound were many very fat, well-fed sheep. The walls of the enclosure were so high and the bars so close together that it was impossible for the sheep or anything to escape once inside. Due to his long fast, however, the wolf was so thin that he knew he could squeeze in through the bars and feast himself on the sheep to his heart's content. Although hunger urged him on, the wily wolf also realized that, after he ate his fill, he would be unable to escape. The wolf sat and pondered and then found an ingenious solution.

What did the wolf do?

				6	8			3
			5		3	2		
		7		1		5	4	
3	1							
6		5		2				
		4					3	2
		6					1	7
						3	6	9
					4			

Can you spot?

We've hidden ten spanners in this garage.
Can you spot them all?

MEDIUM PUZZLES

Word search

```
F S M Z B W J S A F I G U R E
I K C O L C E G N I L R U H K
S A E I K W A T E R P O L O O
H Y T R S C A L S K U D A F R
I A A C E S A R P U A T F T T
N K K A L P O R C I I L C C S
G P S N Y E E R T C N T U K O
T R E O S D R E I R X E S G Z
O G C E R V N K K K C I K N E
O N I I M C S A C E S G E F A
F I J G D R A O B P M N L I B
E V R U E R U U E O K I E N U
R I R T D R O E S O F W T I C
A D A M S G D N S L A O O S S
B W M E D L E Y D J L R N H X
```

ACROSKI	FINISH	ROWING
ALPINE	FISHING	SCISSOR
BANDY	FLOATS	SCUBA
BAREFOOT	HURLING	SKELETON
BOARD	ICE SKATE	SPEED
CANOE	JUDGE	STROKE
CLERK	KAYAK	TIMEKEEPER
CLOCK	KICK	TRACK
COURSE	LUGE	TURNS
CRAWL	MEDLEY	WATER POLO
DIVING	NORDIC	WATER SKI
FIGURE	POOL	WETSUIT

Camp conifer

(57)

Every tree 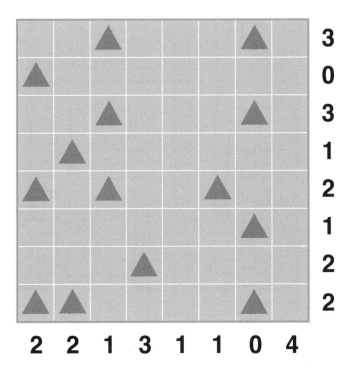 has one tent △ found horizontally or vertically adjacent to it. No tent can be in an adjacent square to another tent (even diagonally). The numbers by each row and column tell you how many tents are there. Can you locate all the tents?

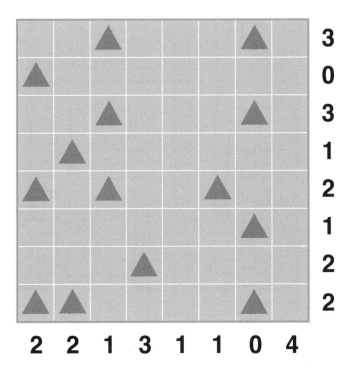

3
0
3
1
2
1
2
2

2   2   1   3   1   1   0   4

Maze

Spot the difference

Can you spot ten differences between this pair of pictures?

Jealousy

A circus troupe is like a large family, and many of the famous names of travelling showmen of the fairgrounds have become part of "Big Top" folklore, to be remembered by children of all ages and never to be forgotten. The history of the circus is dominated by dynasties such as Hagenbeck, the Franconis, the Ringling Brothers and, perhaps the most famous, Barnum and Bailey's Greatest Show on Earth. As in any large family, life in a circus is not always harmonious and tensions are bound to arise from time to time. The story I am about to tell began in one of the smaller establishments.

A typical circus performance in those days consisted of the overture, performing animals, juggling, wire-walking and the flying trapeze. A team of clowns is the icing on the cake, and in our particular story Elsa the female clown was the darling of the audience.

Her vivacity and charm had also captivated Arthur, the conductor of the band, who fell passionately in love with her. In this he was not alone, but had to compete with the attentions of Adrian, the trapeze artist.

The highlight of every evening was the flying trapeze act performed by Adrian and his partner Brian. Both had to swing blindfolded without a safety net and exchange trapezes at a certain moment. Arthur selected this act to eliminate his competitor.

How did he do it without in any way interfering with the equipment?

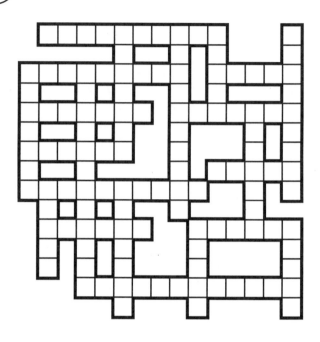

5 letter words
GHOST
INTRO
KORAN
LOUSE
UVULA
YIKES

6 letter words
GATEAU
LAY OUT
THWACK

7 letter words
AUCTION
ITALICS
NOSTRUM
REQUIRE
SKID LID
WOODCUT

9 letter words
NONSMOKER
SUBWOOFER

10 letter words
DISHEARTEN
MALT WHISKY
STRENGTHEN

12 letter words
PROCESSIONAL
WILL-O'-THE-WISP

			5				7	
6	9				4			
		3						
1				6			4	
4	6		3	1	8		5	9
	8			7				1
						2		
			9				3	5
	4				1			

Word search

```
J M A D L L A B R E H T E T K
F O O T B A L L H B N E E R G
G O A L I E E T A L P E M O H
W F T K C O C E L T T U H S H
R R E F E R E E D I K S D B C
E A N W S I L L Y C T L B A T
T C N D E R E L U R E F M S I
T Q I R T C E P I I L O S K P
U U S W U V C K F O M F G E Z
P E D E A N E T G B U F N T R
I T D R B R U M P I R E I B E
R B T B A O P B A V C N N A K
O A U M S U V R H T S S N L N
N L J N E G G E O C C E I L U
C L O V E M A G R P T H P J B
```

BASE	INNINGS	REFEREE
BASKETBALL	IRON	RUN
BAT	LOVE	SCRUM
BUNKER	MATCH	SET
CLUB	NET	SHUTTLECOCK
DEUCE	OFFENSE	SILLY
FOOTBALL	OUTFIELD	STRIKER
GAME	OVER	TEE
GOALIE	PITCH	TENNIS
GOLF	PROP	TETHERBALL
GREEN	PUCK	TRAVEL
GUARD	PUTTER	UMPIRE
HOME PLATE	RACQUET BALL	WOOD

Spot the difference

Can you spot ten differences between this pair of pictures?

2			3	1				9
				4	8	7		
	7	8						6
	2		5					
				7				
					2		3	
8						5	4	
		5	4	9				
1				6	5			7

Word grid

5 letter words
GAMMA
IMBUE
MANIA
SLEEP

6 letter words
SADISM
TRUDGE

7 letter words
BEATNIK
DEWDROP
NIOBIUM

8 letter words
CELLULAR
CROUPIER

9 letter words
BIRDBRAIN
EVERYBODY

10 letter words
BULLHEADED
QUADRUPLET
VELOCIPEDE

12 letter words
NAMBY-PAMBIES
PICK UP THE TAB
TARTARE SAUCE

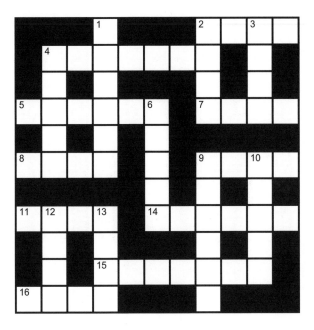

Across

2. Hectic (4)
4. Dud shot (7)
5. Cruel intention (6)
7. Block (4)
8. Fine-tune (4)
9. Spilt the beans (4)
11. Collapse (4)
14. Over there (6)
15. Take part (7)
16. Reveal (4)

Down

1. Resident (6)
2. Superior (4)
3. Glycine max (4)
4. Softly (5)
6. Appreciate (5)
9. Poem (6)
10. Girl, related (5)
12. Turkish currency (4)
13. Speed (4)

Word search

```
S K G T S R H Y G I E A J X G
A E P E U F E K U D K P I M E
E W B L T Z E T R A P I S A N
R S O L U E U D S Z U L F I I
O N E U L O C M K U H L U A U
B O K S P P I A I T A P R T S
S N I D T E L A Y U I E I U O
U R N A A N T T I S N R A W S
S T H Q N A A M E N R A E I U
P P N U U T O Z D Z U N Q I H
Y A I I L E C S E S S U N J L
I B R L W S R I U I K H S E U
X R G O V A S Z R R P X B L H
J X I O L I B E R H O A E W T
O F W S S F A E G I R H N U C
```

AEGIR	FURIAE	MAIA
AMEN-RA	GENIUS	NIKE
ANU	HEL	NQA
APIS	HORUS	PAN
AQUILO	HYGIEA	PENATES
AUSTER	INUUS	PLUTO
BEL	IRUS	PLUTUS
BOREAS	LAR	PTAH
COATLICUE	LIBER	SEB
CTHULHU	LIPS	SOL
EOS	LUA	TELLUS
ERIS	LUNA	TUI
FLORA	MAAT	UPIS

Sudoku

		8						7
9		6			2			
			6		7		5	
				9			1	5
		9		1		8		
3	8			4				
	6		3		1			
			5			2		3
4						1		

The kangaroo court

During the 1950s and 60s a terrorist group active in Germany was trying to destabilize the ruling establishment. One cell, consisting of a young woman and five men, kidnapped a junior official of the Ministry of the Interior.

They held a mock trial, accusing him of being responsible for brutal police tactics, and duly sentenced him to death. One of the terrorists, Hans Helldorf, who had particularly suffered police brutality, volunteered to carry out the execution. He quickly shot the official three times at close range, stepping back to avoid the blood as the man pitched forward. Hans then reached down to check the man's pulse, nodded with satisfaction and the group departed hurriedly.

The next morning, the terrorist murder made the headlines in all the papers. A few days later Helldorf met a highranking police officer in plainclothes and confessed. The policeman made notes, shook hands with Helldorf and departed. Explain.

Crossword

Across

5. Divine glow (4)
6. Pit (6)
7. Putrescence (3)
8. Small river fish (4)
9. Listen in (6)
11. Foe (4)
13. Hard kidney fat (4)
15. Hard work (6)
16. Drinker (4)
18. Amazement (3)
19. Cup holder (6)
20. Shut firmly (4)

Down

1. Indian prince (4)
2. Face-top (8)
3. Eightsome (5)
4. Cable anew (6)
10. Unsettled (8)
12. Lofty (6)
14. Essence (5)
17. Sharp blow (4)

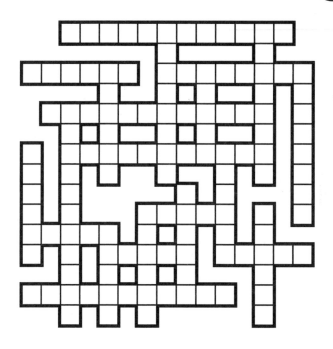

5 letter words
BOSUN
ÉTUDE
NEONS
RERUN
WHEAT
YEARN

6 letter words
BOURSE
BRAZEN
ESTEEM
EVENLY
FAXBAG
FLURRY
KUNG FU

8 letter words
GRACIOUS
INTERNET

11 letter words
BUSINESSMAN
INADVERTENT
NAIL VARNISH

12 letter words
COUNCIL HOUSE
INEXPERIENCE

Spot the difference

Can you spot ten differences between this pair of pictures?

Across

1. Stuffing herb (4)
5. Clever-clogs (4)
7. Flat (9)
8. Lay out (6)
10. Hibernian (4)
11. Honest (4)
13. Bold (6)
15. Unreadable (9)
18. Folio (4)
19. Foot journey (4)

Down

2. Humiliate (5)
3. Slippery (7)
4. Animal companion
5. Litigate (3)
6. Excel (5)
9. Stub (3)
10. Briny cloud (3,4)
12. Indian yoghurt
14. Winnow (5)
16. Pastry-lined dish (3)
17. Brock-house (3)

Sudoku

				3			9	
4							6	5
	3					7	2	
		3			4			
5			2	6	9			3
			7			2		
	9	2					3	
3	7							4
	8			5				

Pit bull terrier

Tom the butcher was trying to deliver a leg of lamb and some sausages to the cottage of Jack the cobbler.

However, there was nobody at home. Somewhat annoyed, Tom was about to turn back when a gust of wind blew his new hat toward Jack's cherry tree. Trying to retrieve it, Tom faced a slight problem. Tied to the tree on a long leash was Kim, the pit bull terrier well-known and feared for his viciousness, and the hat was just within his reach. How could Tom recover his hat without being attacked by Kim?

Spot the difference

Can you spot ten differences between this pair of pictures?

```
T U N G S T E N M U I M S O B
Y P E C Z K P L U R D M C D R
Q N P M U I D N I H L U O S S
Z M T U C R N J R O O N B O I
B E U I A M I C A D G I A D L
Y R N D R N U U B I P M L I V
N C I I B Q O I M U L U T U E
O U U R O C D D T M U L J M R
M R M I N N K T A N T A L U M
I Y T E I R L O F R O L E A D
T I O C Y B X E J X N R V O W
N N K P O Y I E M U I R T T Y
A E T R G U R A N I U M B S I
L O O E H P O B R O M I N E F
N N N H A F N I U M N O G R A
```

ALUMINUM	IRIDIUM	RADON
ANTIMONY	IRON	RHODIUM
ARGON	KRYPTON	SILVER
BARIUM	LEAD	SODIUM
BORON	MERCURY	STRONTIUM
BROMINE	NEON	TANTALUM
CARBON	NEPTUNIUM	TIN
COBALT	NICKEL	TUNGSTEN
CURIUM	OSMIUM	URANIUM
GOLD	OXYGEN	XENON
HAFNIUM	PLUTONIUM	YTTRIUM
INDIUM	RADIUM	ZINC

Matrix

Which of the boxed figures completes the set?

Camp conifer

Every tree ▲ has one tent △ found horizontally or verically adjacent to it. No tent can be in an adjacent square to another tent (even diagonally). The numbers by each row and column tell you how many tents are there. Can you locate all the tents?

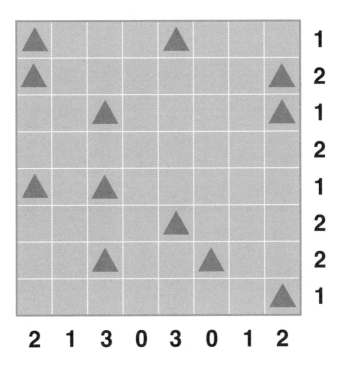

Sudoku

						6	7	
				3				2
9		4		8				
	2				6	1	9	
		9		2		4		
	4	3	7				8	
				4		5		1
8				6				
	6	2						

Crossword

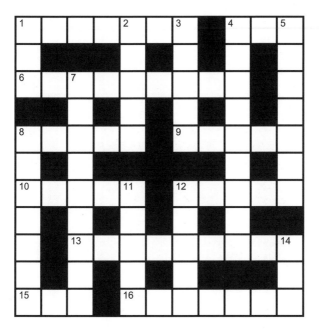

Across

1. Curved sword (7)
4. Street hopper (3)
6. Custom (9)
8. Pulse (5)
9. Wear down (5)
10. Respond (5)
12. Tablet (5)
13. Meddle (9)
15. Tolkeinian tree-creature (3)
16. Juvenile (7)

Down

1. Sever (3)
2. Digression (5)
3. Glow (5)
4. Good trip (3,6)
5. Preeminent (7)
7. Trapeze artist (9)
8. Injector (7)
11. Tally (3,2)
12. Twilled wool (5)
14. Increase (3)

Code grid

25	1	25	1		11	21	3	12	11	18	21	12
4		21		1		11		25		1		9
14	21	7	1	26	12	11		8	22	22	24	4
25		24		14		4		12		1		22
17	24	23	18	5		3	4	1	22	2	8	
24				13		5				8		2
23	4	6	6	8	22		24	22	3	1	4	26
18		4				11		8				21
	2	13	1	20	24	8		1	23	1	11	11
1		13		24		19		26		16		11
10	21	4	13	1		24	23	16	26	1	14	8
21		21		3		1		5		11		5
9	4	22	15	3	1	13	13		14	25	8	8

1	2	3	4	5	6 Z	7	8	9	10	11	12	13
14	15	16	17	18	19	20	21	22	23 M	24	25 H	26

Logic sequence

The balls below have been rearranged. Can you work out the new sequence of the balls from the clues given below?

Neither the triangle nor the X is next to the square.
Neither the triangle nor the X is next to the circle.
Neither the X nor the square is next to the star.
The circle is immediately to the right of the star.

Word grid

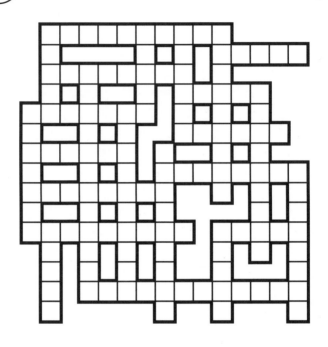

5 letter words
ABOUT
EERIE
RELIC
SCREE
SEDAN
SONNY
XEBEC

6 letter words
ACIDIC
ARRANT
TATTOO

7 letter words
SCRAPPY
SWALLOW

8 letter words
EDGEWAYS
IMMOBILE
LAUREATE
LISTENER

9 letter words
DIETETICS
EXTORTION

TWO-TIMERS
WELL-OILED

10 letter words
PICCALILLI
REAL ESTATE

12 letter words
PRINCIPALITY
STANDARD LAMP

Camp conifer

Every tree 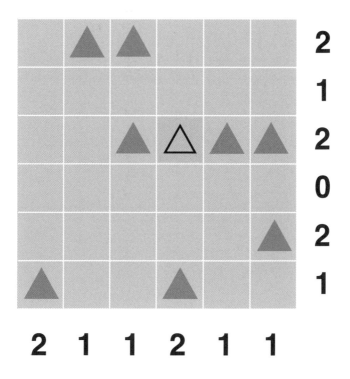 has one tent △ found horizontally or vertically adjacent to it. No tent can be in an adjacent square to another tent (even diagonally!). The numbers by each row and column tell you how many tents are there. Can you locate all the tents?

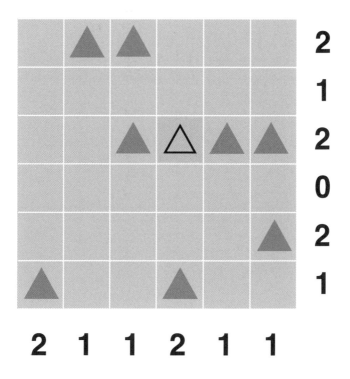

Sudoku

			5		8		7	3
								4
		7			6		9	
				9		3	2	
		5		2		9		
	2	1		7				
	7		4			6		
1								
3	4		1		7			

Word grid

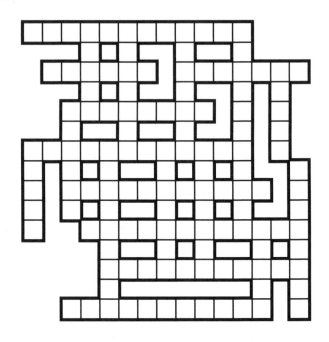

5 letter words
BLAME
FJORD
UMBRA
UNSAY

6 letter words
REBUKE
VOYAGE

7 letter words
AMOROUS
INKLING
OLDSTER
SPASTIC
THORIUM

8 letter words
GREENERY
VALIDATE

9 letter word
NONENTITY

11 letter words
CRYSTALLISE
GIN AND TONIC
INCRIMINATE
PERESTROIKA

12 letter words
FLYING DOCTOR
FREUDIAN SLIP
INEXTRICABLE

More or less

The arrows indicate whether a number in a box is greater or smaller than an adjacent number. Complete the grid so that all rows and columns contain the numbers 1 to 6.

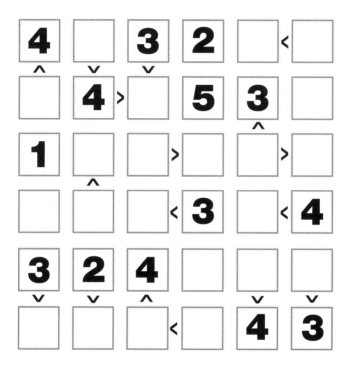

Corners

Use the corners to make the central number the same way in all three cases. What number should replace the question mark?

	9	3					2	
5	2		8					3
					4	1		
				6		3		
			9	3	2			
		8		1				
		6	7					
9					5		1	7
	7					5	6	

Crossword

Across

2. Eternal (7)
6. Sign (7)
7. Amount (3)
8. Suitably (5)
10. Right-hand page (5)
12. Seraglio (5)
15. Proclamation (5)
17. Young lion (3)
18. Ordinary (7)
19. Sac up (7)

Down

1. Hot breakfast (3-2)
3. Brave (5)
4. Madagascan primate (5)
5. Crash (5)
9. Falsehood (3)
11. Finish (3)
13. Blue (5)
14. Giddy (5)
15. Burst out (5)
16. Rabbit (5)

Word search

```
A B D N A L E C I Y N I A B D
S U I Y R R H O O A E D Q M M
U O S Y R I A G P N A M O V P
E K I T L X O A K G G P E R U
A E I E R T J U A U Q O X N Y
U N G T M A L I L I W Z C A E
V Y I B A W L A L N S A C B K
N A N H U L O I Q E N I I W R
O B Y A C S Y H A A A R N T U
Z D E N M A R K R M W E M U T
C Q A R I R D N A L I A H T T
U E M N O M E J T I A G N O T
B R D U O M A G A B T D A H C
A I B R E S A U Q Y A W R O N
A U S T R I A N G A H A I T I
```

AUSTRALIA	INDIA	PERU
AUSTRIA	IRAN	QATAR
CHAD	IRAQ	SERBIA
CHILE	ITALY	SYRIA
CHINA	JAMAICA	TAIWAN
CONGO	JAPAN	THAILAND
CUBA	KENYA	TOGO
DENMARK	KUWAIT	TONGA
GERMANY	LAOS	TUNISIA
GUAM	LIBYA	TURKEY
GUINEA	MALI	USA
HAITI	NORWAY	YEMEN
ICELAND	OMAN	ZAIRE

Riddle

A soldier's dream

A soldier had a dream that his king would be assassinated on his first visit to a foreign city. He pleaded with the King to cancel his visit, thinking the vision might be a horrible omen. The King pondered the man's advice for a moment and then ordered him to be taken away and beheaded.

Why?

Spot the difference

Can you spot ten differences between this pair of pictures?

The Rolls-Royce Corniche

Ronnie Breskal and Ernesto Saler have been friends for many years. Ronnie has reached the pinnacle of his profession, enjoying all the trappings of a successful career – a beautiful house, expensive cars, the lot. Ernesto works in the same industry though much less successfully, at least in terms of financial rewards. Nevertheless Ernesto feels no envy. On the contrary, he admires Ronnie and tries to emulate him in many ways. He often wears similar clothes to Ronnie's and works hard at trying to look like his idol.

One sunny spring morning he takes Ronnie's brand new Rolls-Royce Corniche for a spin. He races along a narrow mountain road and, as he is trying to negotiate a tight bend at excessive speed, loses control and the car catapults into space. Ernesto just manages to jump clear. The Corniche, which was not even insured, becomes a total write-off.

Ronnie, far from being angry, seems slightly amused, congratulates Ernesto and gives it no further thought. Can you explain Ronnie's strange indifference?

Rouge et noir

The scene: A famous Monte Carlo casino. A distinguished gentleman with a stunning brunette at his side is playing red or black at the roulette table. Watching them is another couple nearby. George Benson and Isabelle Labrue start to talk. "You know, Isabelle, I often wonder why Philip Castle continues to play. He loses most of the time – roughly 500,000 francs a year." "He must be very rich," Isabelle offers. "Not really," responds George. "His wife, Deborah, the lovely creature by his side, is the one with the money and she finances him." "She must be very much in love or very stupid, or she would leave him and find someone with better luck." "On the contrary, she is quite happy with the situation," says George, with a knowing smile. Why?

Maze

Word grid

5 letter words
AVERT
EAGER
IRONY
OLDEN
ROSIN
SIREN
SWIPE
THEME

7 letter words
PRECEDE
SATISFY
SLEAZED

9 letter words
EACH OTHER
LACHRYMAL
MILITATES
OURSELVES
SECTARIAN

10 letter words
FLEUR-DE-LIS
FORESHADOW

12 letter words
BULL TERRIERS
HAIR'S-BREADTH
HYPERACIDITY

Sudoku

5		9				4		
		7		2				6
6				4			8	
		5		8	3		2	
2		4		6		8		3
	6		7	5		9		
	2			3				4
9				7		3		
		6				2		8

Word grid

5 letter words
ENVOI
OASIS
RODEO
SIDLE

6 letter words
ENAMEL
MOTIVE

7 letter words
AIRLESS
EMBASSY
LUCERNE
RAIMENT
RUFFIAN
UNMANLY

9 letter words
BOY SCOUTS
SANS SERIF

10 letter words
HORRENDOUS
UNRIVALLED

12 letter words
ARCHITECTURE
CRUSH BARRIER
ONE-UPMANSHIP
UPON MY
    HONOUR

The burglars

John lives with his parents in a large flat in north London. One afternoon, while his parents were out, John was sitting on the sofa with Sophie, the neighbours' daughter, watching television. After a short while, Sophie left to buy some cigarettes. Suddenly two men burst into the flat and, ignoring John, proceeded to take the television set, a tape recorder and a personal computer, and then disappeared.

John had never seen either of the men before, nor was there any legal reason for them to remove the equipment, yet he remained sitting on the sofa throughout the incident without taking any action.

Explain.

Camp conifer

Every tree ▲ has one tent △ found horizontally or verically adjacent to it. No tent can be in an adjacent square to another tent (even diagonally). The numbers by each row and column tell you how many tents are there.

Can you locate all the tents?

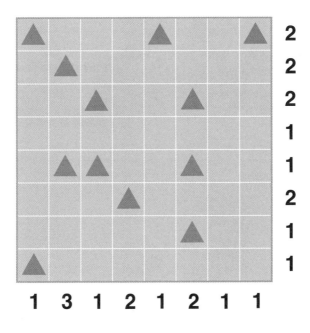

Spot the difference

Can you spot ten differences between this pair of pictures?

Word search

```
S  P  I  R  I  T  X  I  F  C  A  T  T  T  X
Y  E  N  V  R  H  R  N  L  T  U  B  E  E  R
S  Y  V  E  S  I  D  A  I  S  L  U  L  Q  G
Z  W  D  A  S  J  R  E  P  P  H  S  M  V  H
D  I  M  H  R  E  G  Q  A  P  A  H  I  I  F
C  S  T  B  T  G  O  N  V  A  K  E  G  N  A
L  U  A  A  C  E  P  E  A  N  A  R  U  O  W
J  S  E  E  C  H  Y  I  K  H  C  R  X  R  C
S  T  Y  T  S  S  A  U  E  C  C  Y  J  D  B
Y  A  A  T  H  O  U  B  O  S  A  U  Z  I  C
A  V  R  E  R  C  R  M  K  L  L  S  T  N  M
K  A  U  S  U  K  S  A  E  E  W  T  A  A  A
O  C  M  I  B  Q  F  R  P  Y  E  I  J  I  C
T  E  N  N  O  B  U  D  I  R  Z  B  N  R  O
R  A  T  A  F  I  A  G  S  K  C  S  D  E  N
```

ALE	FIX	ROSE
ANISETTE	FLIP	RUM
BASS	GIMLET	RYE
BEER	GRAVES	SACK
BITTERS	IRISH	SCHNAPPS
CAVA	JULEP	SHERRY
CHA	KIRSCH	SHRUB
CIDER	MACON	SMASH
CLARET	MUSCAT	SPIRIT
CRU	NOG	TEA
DRAMBUIE	PEKOE	TOKAY
DUBONNET	RATAFIA	VIN ORDINAIRE

Sudoku

		3			4	5	8	7
		9		8				
	2			3				
		6					3	
			4	2	8			
	9					1		
				5			1	
				4		2		
4	6	5	3			8		

Word grid

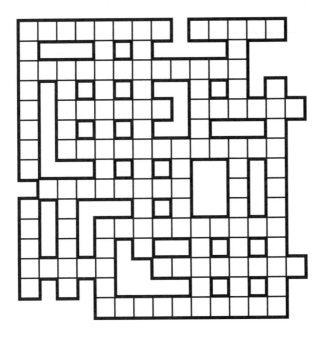

5 letter words
BEADY
CONGA
CRITH
GAMMA
GRASS
LAYER
MANLY
PIN-UP
RUPEE

6 letter words
IMPUGN
NAPERY
OEDEMA

8 letter words
HOSTELRY
PAVEMENT
PIPE RACK
STALLON

9 letter words
HOIPOLLOI
RECIPIENT

10 letter words
GO FOR BROKE
SAFETYPINS

12 letter words
CHANGE OF LIFE
HIEROGLYPHIC
PRECANCEROUS
VICE CHAIRMAN

HARD
PUZZLES

25	1	25	1		11	21	3	12	11	18	21	12
4		21		1		11		25		1		9
14	21	7	1	26	12	11		8	22	22	24	4
25		24		14		4		12		1		22
17	24	23	18	5		3	4	1	22	2	8	
24				13		5				8		2
23	4	6	6	8	22		24	22	3	1	4	26
18		4				11		8				21
	2	13	1	20	24	8		1	23	1	11	11
1		13		24		19		26		16		11
10	21	4	13	1		24	23	16	26	1	14	8
21		21		3		1		5		11		5
9	4	22	15	3	1	13	13		14	25	8	8

| 1 | 2 | 3 | 4 | 5 | 6 Z | 7 | 8 | 9 | 10 | 11 | 12 | 13 |
| 14 | 15 | 16 | 17 | 18 | 19 | 20 | 21 | 22 | 23 M | 24 | 25 H | 26 |

The kidnap

The first ransom demand was made by telephone two days after Eric Watson's disappearance: the kidnappers wanted $3 million in used notes. This was far beyond the family's capability and over the next few days negotiations succeeded in reducing the ransom to $0.5 million dollars.

The police had been involved from the start and had advised the family to insist on tangible proof that Eric was still alive before parting with any money. The following day a photograph was found in the letter-box of Eric holding a copy of the Sun of the previous day.

Detective Inspector O'Reilly was a little sceptical: "This photograph could easily be a fake and needs to be examined by the police laboratory." Two hours later Dr Bernstein, head of the laboratory, handed the photo back to O'Reilly. "This is undoubtedly genuine," he said, "and I have even better news." He whispered something in O'Reilly's ear. The same afternoon the kidnappers' lair was raided and Eric Watson freed.

Explain.

Word search

```
D M Q C N K A R R H E N I U S
I D T L N O I L A K L A D D T
P L I V H I I E E A J N C O Z
A O N M Z N Z T Q D A I O C H
R S Z J R V F H A A I R L W G
J T L A H A V E N R A N E B J
M K O A G R E R X N D T A E V
I U O N R Y C L I I A Y A Y X
A O I N F E D O C D Y T H Y C
C R T R E D N M O U S K E E E
I E Z E U S T I I O N I C M D
M O L E K C N N M M J M E M F
R A Y S L P E U T R I T I U M
S O D A V R R E B A H N T A F
A P Y C T U H X Y F F N E M T
```

ALKALI	FAT	OHM
ANION	HABER	OIL
ARRHENIUS	IMINE	ORE
AZO	INERT	PVC
BUNSEN	INVAR	RAYS
CLAY	IODATE	RING
CURIUM	IONIC	RNA
CYANIDE	KETO	SODA
DDT	META	SOL
DEHYDRATION	MICA	TIN
DNA	MINERAL	TNT
EMF	MOLE	TRITIUM
ETHER	NUCLEAR	ZINC

		4		8		1		
7			2	1	9			3
	2		9		1		8	
				6				
4								1
5	9						7	4
	3						1	
2			7		3			9

Camp conifer

Every tree 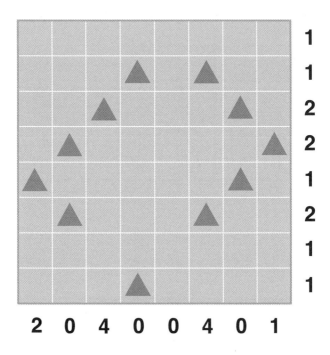 has one tent △ found horizontally or verically
adjacent to it. No tent can be in an adjacent square to another tent
(even diagonally). The numbers by each row and column tell you
how many tents are there.

Can you locate all the tents?

Across

1. Distaff (6)
4. Harsh laugh (4)
6. Reflect (6)
8. British hillside (4)
9. Despatch (4)
10. Rhythm (5)
12. Diacritic (5)
13. Nonsense (4)
15. Select as (4)
17. Shriek (6)
18. Affectation (4)
19. Onus (6)

Down

2. Omit (5)
3. Reduce (7)
4. Food guard (3)
5. Mindful (5)
7. Rachitis (7)
11. Outside cook (7)
12. Petty murderer (5)
14. Trim (5)
16. Lower digit (3)

The fancy-dress ball

Martin Hofmann was a foreign exchange dealer in the Zurich branch of Intertrust AG, a medium-sized private bank. Management decided to arrange a number of social events in addition to the annual Christmas party to promote the team spirit among staff. Martin received an invitation, signed by the manager, to one of these events: a fancy-dress ball at the Baur-Au-Lac, one of the most exclusive five-star hotels in town. The motto for the ball was "A night at the court of Louis XV".

Martin thought long and hard as to what to wear. In the end he hired the outfit of a court jester. When he entered the ballroom he created a minor sensation. Assuming the date, time and venue were all correct, what did he do wrong?

```
D N W R E U M I R C S F D L R
T B S P U O G Z H C X A Q S F
S N N O C O K H O U S E W A Y
U P E B T S B R S C D I P C N
P D I M E T N R I O S U M X O
T L A D U E Z M A D R C E G R
X S S O R R P A Y T E H R C I
K R T H U E T L E F L A T A J
Q U L O T X F S L O L N D N V
C S L K F I R U N P E C A S T
D L A I T M N U R I V R D R A
A E C H O R E O G R A P H E R
T X C B C U L I T T R V E T L
Z A D K F K O I I E T I V T X
P W H R W Z B P P F S U E V B
```

ARBOUR	DIM	MIC
CALL	DIPS	MIXER
CANS	DSR	NOTES
CAST	ERS	OP
CHOREOGRAPHER	FLAT	PIT
CORNER	FLY	RUN
CSI	FX	SCRIM
CUE	GO UP	SET
CUT-OUT	HOUSE	TRAVELLER
DAT	INSTRUMENT	USL
DBO	IRON	USR
DECK	LX	WAY
DESK	MASK	XLR

	26		8		25		2		1		12	
1	5	9	10	25	5		1	6	5	22	5	21
	12		9		18		21		19		26	
19	12	14	9		11	5	16	19	25	8	16	4
			14		5		19		14		9	
10	24	14	12	14	2	22		9	12	5	16	9
	2				22		1				5	
8	12	10	7	14		1	25	16	13	5	18	21
	16		10		26		15		10			
1	2	23	9	3	16	19	6		6	5	8	8
	23		16		21		16		23		17	
10	19	22	2	24	14		20	14	23	16	5	1
	14		19		9		6		15		4	

| 1 | 2 | 3 | 4 | 5 | 6 | 7 | 8 | 9 D | 10 | 11 | 12 | 13 |
| 14 | 15 | 16 I | 17 | 18 | 19 | 20 | 21 | 22 | 23 | 24 | 25 K | 26 |

Looplink

Connect adjacent dots with either horizontal or vertical lines to create a continuous unbroken loop which never crosses over itself. Some (but not all) of the boxes contain numbers revealing exactly how many sides of that box are occupied by your unbroken line.

3	1		2		2
	2	2	2	2	2
2	1		3	3	
2	1	2	2	2	2
	2		2		1
3	1	2	3	1	0

The fatal bullet

Mario Franchesci was deeply troubled. He was infatuated with his girlfriend Sylvia and could not accept the thought that she would have to die. There was proof that Sylvia had broken the strict law of Omerta, never to betray the Cosa Nostra – she had been observed entering the DA's office in disguise.

The conclusion was clear. The Capo di Tutti Capi had instructed Mario to eliminate her. Mario had resisted, and as a consequence his own position was in jeopardy.

As he paced up and down in his study, chain-smoking, he knew in his heart of hearts that he would have to do the deed. He walked two blocks to Sylvia's apartment and opened the door with his own key. He tiptoed into her bedroom. Sylvia was asleep. Mario looked at her with a mixture of love and anguish. He held the gun close to her temple and pulled the trigger. It felt as if he had shot himself.

Two days later he was arrested. Mario had been careless. The gun was still in his possession and forensics had no difficulty in establishing that the bullet had come from it. Surprisingly, however, Mario was released the same afternoon, all charges against him having been dropped.

Explain.

Where's the pair?

Only two of these pictures are exactly the same. Can you spot the matching pair?

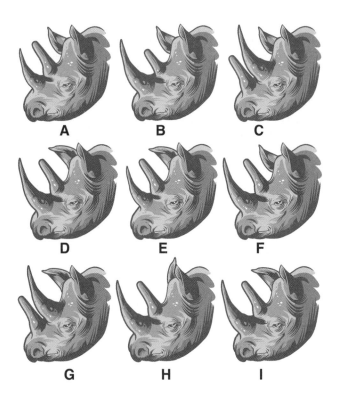

```
B B E Z P J S K F M D M R F F
S S R T U G D Q R F D C R L L
U Y U E E S U T C A C E K M O
G A C L G J M A M M E O E O W
A J T D D A K O T A S H A C E
R O X C T N Y Y N E T A Q O R
H L J U A H A O H T C T X P D
I S E L B R A M V S 2 W O O R
L F W T H F Q E J V U S F T N
L M V H S E N Q A M E R D L O
G R A P A T O U S E T A R I P
A Z C G U M Q E G O E X A P O
N U L R N C R E D S W D W R U
G E E G D U E N U H A Q H F H
S S G R Q B M M R D A Z O T U
```

ACE	HOTLEGS	RUSH
A-HA	KFMDM	SAXON
BEE GEES	KLF	STEAM
CACTUS	MAGNUM	SUGARHILL GANG
CCR	MAN	THEM
CULT	MARBLES	TOTO
CURE	OJAYS	UFO
DADA	PIL	VENTURES
DAKOTAS	PIRATES	VOYAGER
DIO	POCO	WHAM
EAGLES	QUEEN	WHO
FREE	REM	WOLF

Code grid

	17		20		17		9		9		16	
17	4	6	13	22	25		26	13	26	14	21	7
	13		22		7		22		22		3	
4	21	23	17		12	23	12	16	21	12	17	25
			6		26		7		15		22	
3	9	6	2	21	3	1		13	15	15	3	1
	10				1		1				12	
20	3	1	20	6		10	3	4	8	13	23	11
	1		12		17		25		13			
24	1	12	5	5	3	22	19		26	3	7	9
	7		12		9		13		14		1	
26	13	11	6	23	17		18	13	6	15	21	1
	2		22		25		23		25		10	

1 L	2	3	4	5	6	7	8	9	10	11	12	13
14	15	16	17	18	19	20 V	21 U	22	23	24	25	26

Across

6. More (5)
7. My private state (5)
8. Ballet step (3)
10. Refreshment parlour (7)
11. Obedient (7)
13. Fiasco (7)
15. Assist (3)
16. Chutzpah (5)
17. Flowery position (5)

Down

1. Glorious (11)
2. Drumstoke sounds (3-3)
3. Opera singer (4)
4. Warrior's Heaven (8)
5. Sound source (7, 4)
9. Mutton chop (8)
12. Weak (6)
14. Man (4)

Sudoku

		4		8		6		3
		3	7	5				
5	6							
	5		6		7		9	
9	2			1				
			9			3		
7					8	5		
			3				1	8
4							3	7

Only one of these pictures is an exact mirror image of the first one. Can you spot it?

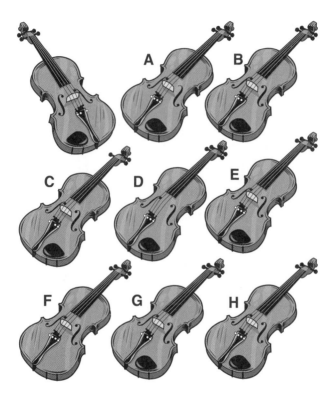

Small logic

As a warm-up for the 2012 Olympics, East London held three competitions in Martial Arts, Tennis and Football. Can you work out from these clues where each sport was held and at which venue, and which country won each event?

1) The tennis in Hackney was not held in the gardens or won by a Spaniard
2) Italy won the martial arts contest, not in White City
3) The venue in Lewisham was the town green

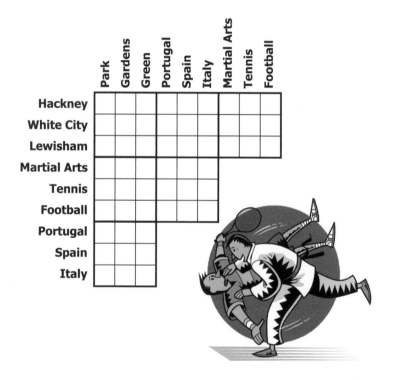

Riddle

The invention

He was known as Ollie though nobody knew, or for that matter
cared, whether it was his first or last name. Ollie was a professional
inventor. Come to him with a problem and he would design a
suitable gadget to solve it.

One day he was approached with a rather unusual request. His
customer needed a telephone and loudspeaker system which would
receive calls, store them in a memory and resend them through the
loudspeaker system after an interval of precisely five minutes, the
set to be operated by remote control. If not switched on, the system
would work like a standard telephone connection. Unusual but
not very difficult, Ollie thought, and using microchips the system
was designed within a few hours. The £500 he received as a fee was
considered "money for jam". Two months later he was arrested and
accused of fraud, though eventually he would clear his name.

Explain the reason for his arrest.

Sudoku

	7		5		6	8		
2	1			9	8			
								5
1					2	7		3
	3			7	9			
4	8		1	5				
7			8			2	4	
						3		
		3	9					6

Use the corners to make the central number the same way in all three cases. What number should replace the question mark?

Where's the pair?

Only two of the shapes below are exactly the same. Can you find the matching pair?

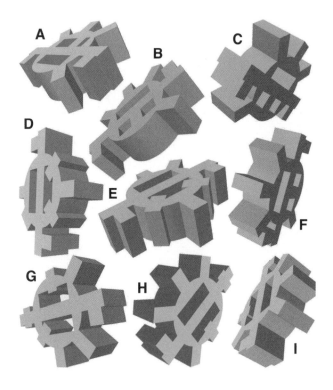

Crossword

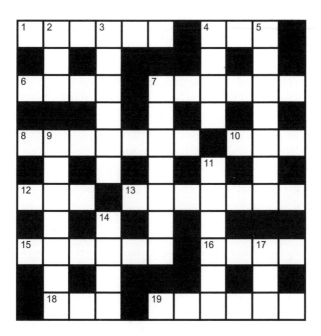

Across

1. Server (6)
4. Rummy (3)
6. Formerly (4)
7. Priest-doctor (6)
8. Moistureless (4-3)
10. Moggy
12. Possesses (3)
13. Gibber (7)
15. Come together (6)
16. Location (4)
18. Illuminated (3)
19. Prison boss (6)

Down

2. Grassy beard (3)
3. With motif (6)
4. Spline (4)
5. Beverage biscuit (7)
7. Notched (7)
9. Ongoing fluke (2, 1, 4)
11. German chief (6)
14. Timing (4)
17. Golf stand (3)

The vandal

A rough-looking stranger enters a restaurant with a sledgehammer. He selects one of two identical pieces of equipment and, without warning, smashes it into fragments. He then walks out without uttering a word. The restaurant owner is not surprised. In fact, he seems to have expected the visit and makes no attempt to interfere. However, after the visitor leaves, the owner makes one telephone call, as a result of which the body of the stranger is discovered next morning in a ditch outside town. What has happened?

	7							9
			6	3				
		4				8		
					2			
2			5				1	
9	3			6			7	
	4	5				1		
		2	8					4
			3	2				

The mountain

Ali lived in a very beautiful little village nestled in a valley in southern Turkey. An avid mountain-climber, every weekend he climbed the nearby mountain. However, although he was a very proficient climber, he always turned back just before he reached the peak. Why?

Word search

```
E D Q H R R M D N H T D M E M
D R R E G N I S K S Y T A R A
A L X N U O V C Z X E Q C Y D
G X H E N E N T J F M N D L Q
K V J S Y R N G E I S X O H X
U I K C H O Z A D N Y N W J P
G O Y O M O G N I R R I E L W
O L E G W M I L H A U D L M I
L A E N A M D L E F Q M L A S
D S D D M I U C N O J L L E L
M F O H E R H A D L U O G S A
A Z B R K P G O R K C N D T M
R I A B C R Z H L I O O B O E
K B S T O M K I N S D N A S Y
C P S Y L A D O K R T S X O X
```

AIR	GOULD	NICOLAI
ARNOLD	HOLST	NONO
BASS	ISLAMEY	OBOE
BAX	JIG	ORGAN
CUI	JONES	PED
DIM	KODALY	RING
EGMONT	LOCKE	SEGNO
ENESCO	LYRE	SFZ
FELDMAN	MACDOWELL	SINGER
FOLK	MAESTOSO	SOR
GADE	MAW	TEN
GOLDMARK	MILHAUD	TOMKINS
GONG DRUM	MOORE	VIOLA

Attica

The prisoners were assembled in the mess hall for dinner. Two of the most feared inmates, Jaime Sanchez and Moses Washington, were engaged in a heated discussion about the spiralling violence between their rival factions.

Both men had started their adult life with great promise. Jaime's parents always thought that their son would follow his father into the medical profession and had spared no expense to put him through medical school. Things started to go very wrong when Jaime began to take drugs, and very soon he was completely out of control, becoming involved in drug-pushing and eventually murder.

Moses, on the other hand, had trained to be a priest but had allowed himself to be influenced by his old friends, who were all members of street gangs. Very soon his religious vocation went out of the window and he became even more vicious and ruthless than the rest of the gang. Moses glared maliciously across the table at Jaime and called him a vile name. Jaime responded by making crude comments about Moses' parents.

Suddenly Moses' face turned purple and he gripped Jaime's arm like a vice. Jaime immediately struck Moses a fearful blow with his fist, then produced from somewhere a vicious-looking handmade knife and stuck it into Moses, who fell forward onto the table, bleeding profusely. The guards quickly moved in and Moses was rushed to the infirmary.

The next day Jaime was brought to visit Moses in the hospital. When Moses saw Jaime he took him warmly by the hand, thanked him and promised that he would never call him names again.

Explain.

Homicide

Peter Collins stood accused of murder in the first degree. He pleaded self-defence, claiming he had been attacked by the victim with a kitchen knife. Evidence, one way or the other, was purely circumstantial and so, after some hectic plea-bargaining, a guilty plea of manslaughter was accepted and Collins was sentenced for three to seven years. In prison, Collins found himself sharing a cell with a contract killer working for the Mafia, who had got away with a two-year sentence for possession of an offensive weapon, a handgun, without a licence.

A few months later, when the two men had become friendly, Collins confessed to his cellmate that he had got away with manslaughter but had in fact committed the murder at the request of a crime syndicate. With an air of professional pride, his cellmate, in turn, told Peter in detail about his own several contract killings. Perhaps Peter's syndicate might use the Mafia man's services too when he was released?

Some time later Peter Collins was transferred to another prison. Then a petition by his lawyer to the governor of the state was granted and Collins was released from prison, having served only five months of his sentence.

Explain how.

Riddle

Lost

Eight-year-old Bobby, obviously lost, was running down Baker Street looking frantically left and right for John. People looked at him sympathetically but no one offered to help. Suddenly he stopped dead in his tracks as he heard a familiar noise, although nobody else in the street seemed to hear it. immediately he turned round and ran excitedly in the direction he had originally come from. Soon he was reunited with John. Explain.

The claquers

Theatre directors in pre-war Vienna used to employ the services of young people, mostly students, to attend performances and demonstrate by repeated and enthusiastic hand-clapping and other gestures that the play was an undoubted success. Paid clappers in French are called les claques, hence the name. In addition to free entry, the claquers also receive a modest payment at the end of the performance.

One evening a French farce by Feydeau was on the programme and the manager selected 12 young men from around 30 who had queued for the job. They waited for about 10 minutes after curtain-up before starting their work. At first it was subdued laughter and clapping at every opportune moment. Then two of them, hoping for a bonus, shouted: "Funny, funny, funny," and finished off with a prolonged belly laugh. The audience did not apparently share the mirth of the claquers. In fact hissing noises were heard from time to time. The team ended their assignment with a roar of laughter and wild clapping just before curtain-down.

After the performance and back at the office to collect their bonus they found instead an irate theatre director who refused to pay and a contrite manager who had been dismissed.

Why?

Word search

```
C H T F E T R O N Y I R F Í C
U V A N I É I A W N U U Y U S
A Ñ P M T C R S S S O H C E P
T N A A I I H A O E F H M N N
R O S P Z G M E D Z A S E R F
O V T O A A A K R R R S Y O U
C E E S J A Q V A O C A E R E
I C L I S O V D Z J U O G R R
E I P R E O I V E U C I Í L T
N E D E U T I C I J H P U U E
T N O T A L P D P G A A Q N B
O T Í Z E A A U N H R V S E O
S O T J G Z V T Y I A O E S B
H S O T A R E A A J D C W L T
K S S N Q M I D M O A W U T A
```

AMIGA	INDIO	PLATO
APIO	LATA	SÍ
CUATROCIENTOS	LEJOS	SOPA
CUCHARADA	LISO	SUR
CUCHARADITA	LUNES	TAREA
DOS	NARIZ	TÉ
ESQUÍ	NORTE	TÍO
FEO	NOVECIENTOS	TIZA
FICHERO	OJO	TRES
FRESA	PASTEL	UÑA
FUERTE	PECHO	UNO
GARZOS	PIEZA	UVA
HIJO	PIJAMA	VELA

Crossword

Across

1. Cunningly (5)
4. Thin, crisp disk (5)
7. Visage (4)
8. Military sack (3,3)
9. Produce (6)
10. Crepuscular lepidopteran (4)
11. Mountain valley (4)
13. Demand (6)
16. Rectangular groove (6)
18. Spell (4)
19. Persian prophet (5)
20. Slammer (5)

Down

2. Hire (5)
3. Fief-holder (5)
5. Creative product (3)
6. Raise up (5)
8. For the fairest (8)
12. Humpless South American camel (5)
14. Stiff rope fibre (5)
15. Summon forth (5)
17. Adieu (3)

The cemetery

In the early post-war period – Vienna – the capital of Austria – had run out of space for additional cemeteries. The Allied bombing and the advancing Red Army had increased the demand for burial space, and the local administration established by the occupying powers tried to find a solution. Several choices were considered. Legislating for compulsory cremation was voted down. Replacing existing graves over 100 years old caused a storm of indignation from the church and the descendants.

Finally one member came up with a bright idea. Can you do so as well?

		7				3		1
			3		9			
3	9			8				2
	6	8					3	
				1		6		
	3		6				1	
					5			7
			2		6	5		
5						4		

Word search

```
O E G N N I A G R A C E Y S J
P N L N O K U Y M T Y M E Q O
U M O I O E B A R V X M S G R
D U E S N K Z P O A A O I A D
F R R E D O E L Q H D S N N A
P R R L N U G M T I P R E G N
G A L B N A H E N I E S Y E A
C Y R E V I R N E E R G E S D
E H U A N G G T I G R I S U A
G V B Z N O Y E L L O W C D N
N C A A B A H H R H I N E N U
A O N R E V I R E T I H W I B
R N G E Z T G N A Y L E N A E
O G I I Q P Y D D A W A R R I
C O L O R A D O Z A M B E Z I
```

AMAZON	ORANGE	SEINE
COLORADO	PARANA	SOMME
CONGO	PO	SYR DARYA
DANUBE	RHINE	THAMES
ELBE	RHONE	TIGRIS
GANGES	MEKONG	UBANGI
GREEN RIVER	MURRAY	VOLGA
HUANG	NIAGRA	WHITE RIVER
HUDSON	NIGER	YANGTZE
INDUS	NILE	YELLOW
IRRAWADDY	OB	YENISEY
JORDAN	ODER	YUKON
LENA		ZAMBEZI

	7		9		3		1	
			8		5			
		3		6		7		
		1				6		
				5				
5	6			1			3	4
2		5	4		7	9		3
		8				1		
	4						8	

11	22	18	23	13	14	16		17	14	17	8	2
5		22		8		2		5		9		9
12	22	15	5	25		14	13	12	9	5	13	3
25		1		5		6				6		14
18	7	3		1	8	4	23	6	22	4	14	2
				14		8		9		8		1
10	5	10	5	17	8		14	26	26	13	14	3
14		9		2		17		2				
4	8	6	1	8	6	14	13	3		25	9	25
7		21				6		24		13		8
11	9	5	16	23	1	3		9	20	9	22	11
14		22		14		14		6		9		14
19	14	2	2	3		6	8	8	11	26	5	2

1	2	3	4	5	6 N	7	8	9 O	10 J	11	12	13
14	15	16	17	18	19	20	21	22	23	24	25	26

Crossword

Across

7. Conscious (5)
8. Stop (5)
9. Ridiculous (5)
10. Upstanding (5)
12. Idea (7)
18. Ancient Mexican (5)
21. Not needed (5)
22. Portrayal (5)
23. Good with jam (5)

Down

1. Chicane (5)
2. Initiate (6)
3. Forbidding (6)
4. Story (4)
5. Enervate (4)
6. Basil sauce (5)
11. Secale cereal (3)
13. Chromaticity (3)
14. Oppose (6)
15. Flowery field (6)
16. Homeless urchin (5)
17. See off (5)
19. Bluish green (4)
20. Musical notation (4)

Word search

```
D O P K M R U S Y T E Y L Z Z
E H C P J C D I R B R A G E R
D O S H O E R L W E T I I F O
S G S L I A T H J A B C K B M
V L N E S O H Q M R Q B O S P
Q Q L O M I D D Y B L O U S E
T O G A R F Y H B O W L E R R
T B T F R A N O R A K M G T S
R L I C H E S T E R F I E L D
O E E B O R V B D A V N V I O
U A T B M C U O Z K R I H K O
S I S S P I I F S K Z M S A H
E L Y M L N C A F O L T U O T
R N I T F U M N R F O Q I F R
S M C P Q T P T S H I R T J F
```

ANORAK	KILT	SKIRT
BELT	MASK	SLIP
BIB	MIDDY BLOUSE	SOCK
BOWLER	MINI	SUIT
BRA	MUFTI	TAILS
CHESTERFIELD	OVERALL	TAM
DERBY	ROBE	TOGA
EARMUFF	ROMPERS	TROUSERS
FEZ	RUBBERS	T-SHIRT
GARB	RUFF	TUNIC
HAT	SARI	ULSTER
HOOD	SARONG	VISOR
HOSE	SHOE	VIZOR

4	8	15	17		3	19	17	16	16	2	8	9
24		22		24		17		9		22		6
10	24	11	13	18	24	25		4	17	18	24	19
8		8		12		18		24		18		2
19	22	7	1	17		19	8	11	13	22	5	
22				1		2				16		22
11	21	22	5	7	23		14	9	24	21	8	6
24		11				17		5				5
	12	17	1	7	17	20		26	24	7	16	8
24		3		8		21		9		1		4
6	1	8	25	5		24	15	1	22	8	1	22
17		24		6		19		19		9		5
16	22	7	9	24	7	17	18		16	7	24	2

1	2	3	4	5	6	7 T	8	9	10	11	12 V	13
14	15	16	17	18 D	19	20	21	22	23	24	25	26

The assassin

When Tessino, the Consigliori to the Vito Bracci family, was found shot dead in his car, no one was surprised. It was an open secret that Tessino had skimmed the profits from the Ritz Casino when he was temporarily in charge of one of the most profitable ventures in the Bracci empire; it was equally certain that Vito Bracci or one of his henchmen was responsible. But suspecting or even knowing, and proving, are two different things.

The facts surrounding the crime were quite unusual. Tessino was killed by three shots, one of which demolished his expensive wristwatch, so that the time of the shooting, 7.34 p.m., could be accurately established. At that time the area surrounding Tessino's limousine was crowded, yet nobody appeared to have heard the shots or noticed the murder.

Can you think of an explanation?

Across

5. By the way (7)
8. Life code (3)
9. Petrified clay (5)
10. Heliopsis (5)
11. Notwithstanding (3)
12. Pismire (3)
13. Gremlin (3)
15. Spread (5)
17. Personal assistant (5)
18. Fuss (3)
19. Patio (7)

Down

1. Quaggy (6)
2. Summit (6)
3. Sharpness (4)
4. Redeem (4)
6. Rife (9)
7. Buzz bomb (6, 3)
13. Aromatic and leafy (6)
14. Bleak (6)
15. Ring (4)
16. Draggy (4)

Code grid

2	10	13	8	4	14	23		20	19	15	9	11
13		20		25		16		4		1		9
15	10	13	14	26	13	11	19	1	24	4	1	17
9		1		19		11				17		23
14	4	23		10	13	4	17	22	9	13	26	13
		13		19		24		4		16		15
8	16	14	17	25	13		11	1	13	14	3	18
13		26		9		21		4		9		
17	4	18	2	26	10	19	19	25		19	16	1
13		13				26		18		14		16
7	13	6	13	17	5	16	13	2	15	9	19	14
9		9		9		14		9		2		16
25	13	15	16	22		17	13	2	12	15	19	22

1	2	3	4	5 Q	6	7	8	9	10	11	12	13
14	15	16	17	18	19	20	21	22	23	24	25 L	26 C

```
E A I C D L O M A S S T A T E
Y L X R Z J W R M B C S Y V G
P B O J O Y E T R M H B A A E
S F I N A Q N O N N O T R A W
J A S R J M W H L M R I G E Q
O O N C N N I A A L U T X N C
N B A I O E H S R O T I Z L H
E V U T M T Y S S A T A R I A
S J O H N S T O N I I N A M U
O F T O O K G B S E L R A H C
S P A R K R L D L T E L C L E
E R A P O A A D Y E B B A S R
V E F E N N E C A S O R B H R
D E L D T R Y A E E E V Z Z C
Z B R E W H I E U S D E N P V
```

ABBEY	CHARLES	LOMAS
AE	CHAUCER	MILNE
AI	CLARE	MUIR
AMIS	DANTE	NORTJE
ASH	ELDER	OWEN
BACA	EUSDEN	PYE
BEER	FORD	ROSA
BELITT	GRAY	SCOTT
BIRNEY	HORACE	SPARK
BLAND	JOHNSTON	TATE
BREW	JONES	THORPE
BROWN	JONSON	TITIAN
CHALLIS	LEE	WARTON

Riddle

The specialist shop

Henry Miller went into a shop which sells several types of one item in daily use. They all serve the same purpose, but some he could take with him if he purchased, while another type would have to be delivered. Even more surprising is the fact that some of the items have more than 1,000 moving components, some have less than 10 and some, believe it or not, have no moving parts whatsoever.

What is the item?

Sudoku

		7	2	9				
		6				2	5	
5	1			4			8	
			6		2			
		5				3		7
2					1			4
				7			3	2
						1		
9			5			4		

Across

2. Girdle (4)
4. Virtuosity (7)
5. Doggy (6)
7. Satisfy (4)
8. Drug (4)
9. Figure out (4)
11. Fustian (4)
14. American (6)
15. Constrict (7)
16. European goat monster (4)

Down

1. Oceanic (6)
2. Without (4)
3. Lampblack (4)
4. British comic (5)
6. Betimes (5)
9. Evening's cue (6)
10. Military blockade (5)
12. Tibetan priest (4)
13. Pipe (4)

The numbers in some squares in the grid indicate the exact number of black squares that should surround it. Shade these squares until all the numbers are surrounded by the correct number of black squares.

			1		2	2			
3		4	3		3				3
2	3			3		2	2	1	1
		2	3		3		3		1
2	3	3		3					2
1				3		4	5	4	
2	4	5					3		2
1			3	2		3		2	1
	5		2	2		5		4	2
		2		1					

Code grid

21	25	7	1	5	3	23		8	21	14	14	7
19		16		16		10		1		6		8
22	10	20	8	6	3	5	3	24		1	16	24
3				6		16		10		7		3
6	1	24	5	1		7	10	19	3	26	10	2
		3		15		26				22		21
22	16	6	6	3	11		15	1	13	21	19	17
10		16				11		23		6		
6	16	18	21	3	14	4		12	1	22	10	11
16		21		6		17		21				10
5	16	1		10	25	16	10	25	7	9	16	25
1		24		17		7		8		3		15
24	26	4	19	3		11	3	11	1	25	21	7

| 1 | 2 | 3 | 4 | 5 V | 6 L | 7 | 8 | 9 | 10 | 11 | 12 | 13 |
| 14 | 15 | 16 | 17 | 18 | 19 | 20 | 21 | 22 | 23 | 24 R | 25 | 26 |

Across

1. Problem (5)
4. Bet (5)
8. Moniker (4)
9. Foreign parts (6)
10. Solid (8)
13. Aesthetic (8)
15. Case (6)
16. Furrow (4)
17. Pry (5)
18. Little hammer (5)

Down

2. Period (6)
3. Purpose (3)
5. Vacuum (7)
6. Test (4)
7. Geographical dictionary (9)
11. Poison (7)
12. Oceanic bandit (6)
14. Food (4)
16. Watering hole (3)

ANSWERS

Puzzle 1

Puzzle 2

8	6	4	9	2	1	5	7	3
5	3	1	8	7	6	2	9	4
9	7	2	4	5	3	6	1	8
7	9	8	3	6	5	4	2	1
1	5	3	2	8	4	9	6	7
4	2	6	1	9	7	8	3	5
2	1	5	7	4	9	3	8	6
6	8	7	5	3	2	1	4	9
3	4	9	6	1	8	7	5	2

Puzzle 3

In his younger days Robert Blocker suffered a compound fracture in one of his legs while skiing in Scotland. The bone pieces had to be fastened together with metal rods and plates. The security detector checks at the airports would be set off every time he passed them, and the x-ray films were needed to explain the reason.

Puzzle 5

Puzzle 6

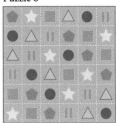

Answers

Puzzle 7

Puzzle 8

8	3	9	5	6	1	4	2	7
1	7	5	3	2	4	9	6	8
4	6	2	8	9	7	1	5	3
9	2	6	4	7	8	3	1	5
3	8	1	9	5	2	7	4	6
7	5	4	1	3	6	8	9	2
5	1	8	2	4	3	6	7	9
2	4	7	6	8	9	5	3	1
6	9	3	7	1	5	2	8	4

Puzzle 9

18	13	14
11	15	19
16	17	12

Puzzle 10

Puzzle 11

7	4	3	1	9	8	6	5	2
6	9	5	7	2	4	3	8	1
1	8	2	3	6	5	9	4	7
2	1	4	5	3	7	8	6	9
8	3	9	2	1	6	5	7	4
5	6	7	4	8	9	1	2	3
3	2	6	8	7	1	4	9	5
9	5	1	6	4	2	7	3	8
4	7	8	9	5	3	2	1	6

Puzzle 12

Puzzle 13

Puzzle 15

Answers

Puzzle 16

8	5	7	3	2	1	6	4	9
4	6	1	5	7	9	8	3	2
3	2	9	4	8	6	7	5	1
1	4	3	8	6	5	9	2	7
6	9	2	7	1	4	5	8	3
7	8	5	2	9	3	1	6	4
5	1	6	9	4	2	3	7	8
2	3	8	1	5	7	4	9	6
9	7	4	6	3	8	2	1	5

Puzzle 17

Puzzle 18

Inspector Garcia had noticed that Gert had a white mark on his ring finger, whereas his arm was uniformly tanned and showed no mark where the Rolex had supposedly been.

Puzzle 19

6	5	9	4	8	1	7	3	2
7	4	3	9	2	5	8	6	1
8	2	1	6	7	3	4	9	5
1	8	2	3	4	9	6	5	7
3	7	6	2	5	8	1	4	9
5	9	4	7	1	6	3	2	8
4	1	7	5	3	2	9	8	6
2	6	8	1	9	4	5	7	3
9	3	5	8	6	7	2	1	4

Puzzle 21

Puzzle 22

3	2	4	8	9	6	5	1	7
7	5	1	3	4	2	6	9	8
6	9	8	7	5	1	4	2	3
5	7	6	4	3	9	2	8	1
9	8	2	1	6	7	3	4	5
1	4	3	2	8	5	7	6	9
4	6	9	5	7	8	1	3	2
8	1	5	6	2	3	9	7	4
2	3	7	9	1	4	8	5	6

Puzzle 23

Answers

Puzzle 25

Puzzle 24

Puzzle 27

Puzzle 26

Puzzle 28
F and H are the pair.

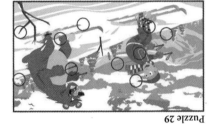

Puzzle 29

Puzzle 30
B and G are the pair.

Puzzle 31

Puzzle 32
They are part of triplets.

Puzzle 33

Answers

Puzzle 34

Puzzle 35
Flutter is fairy D.

Puzzle 36

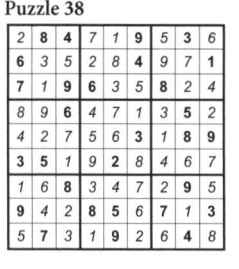

Puzzle 37
He let the air out of the truck's tyres.

Puzzle 38

2	8	4	7	1	9	5	3	6
6	3	5	2	8	4	9	7	1
7	1	9	6	3	5	8	2	4
8	9	6	4	7	1	3	5	2
4	2	7	5	6	3	1	8	9
3	5	1	9	2	8	4	6	7
1	6	8	3	4	7	2	9	5
9	4	2	8	5	6	7	1	3
5	7	3	1	9	2	6	4	8

Puzzle 39
He puts down 4 x 50p coins. If he had required Jubilee he would have put down 3 x 50p coins.

Puzzle 40

Puzzle 41
Answer: 15
Multiply the number of letters in the name of each city by three, and subtract 1 for each vowel.

18 – 3 = 15

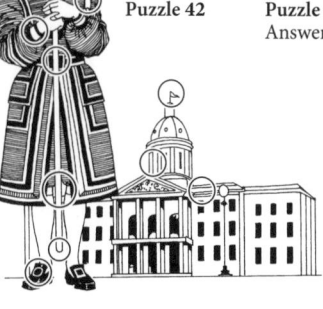

Puzzle 42

Puzzle 43
Answer: A, B and D.

Answers

Puzzle 44

6	7	4	2	5	9	1	8	3
5	3	2	7	1	8	9	4	6
1	9	8	3	4	6	7	2	5
8	2	7	1	9	5	3	6	4
4	5	1	6	3	2	8	9	7
3	6	9	8	7	4	5	1	2
9	4	6	5	8	7	2	3	1
2	1	5	9	6	3	4	7	8
7	8	3	4	2	1	6	5	9

Puzzle 45

The man's son had been on a dialysis machine for years and his condition was deteriorating. Now his only partially working kidney was found to have a malignant growth and had to be removed. Although the doctors still hoped to find a suitable donor for a transplant, the father decided not to risk further delay.

Puzzle 46

Puzzle 47

Puzzle 49

2	5	6	1	7	4	9	8	3
7	3	4	9	8	2	1	5	6
8	9	1	3	5	6	7	4	2
5	4	2	6	1	9	8	3	7
3	7	8	4	2	5	6	9	1
6	1	9	8	3	7	5	2	4
1	2	3	7	9	8	4	6	5
4	8	7	5	6	3	2	1	9
9	6	5	2	4	1	3	7	8

Puzzle 51

Answers

Puzzle 52

Puzzle 53

The wolf squeezed through the bars, killed as many sheep as he thought necessary, tore them into small pieces and pushed them through the bars. He followed through and ate his fill at leisure outside the compound. Some time later, in a Mensa IQ test, the wolf scored 161.

Puzzle 54

5	2	1	4	6	8	9	7	3
4	6	9	5	7	3	2	8	1
8	3	7	2	1	9	5	4	6
3	1	2	9	4	6	7	5	8
6	8	5	3	2	7	1	9	4
7	9	4	1	8	5	6	3	2
9	5	6	8	3	2	4	1	7
2	4	8	7	5	1	3	6	9
1	7	3	6	9	4	8	2	5

Puzzle 55

Puzzle 56

Puzzle 57

△		▲	△			▲	△	3
▲								0
		△	▲	△		▲	△	3
		▲			△			1
▲	△	▲	△		▲			2
						▲	△	1
△			▲	△				2
▲	▲	△				▲	△	2
2	2	1	3	1	1	0	4	

Puzzle 59

Answers

Puzzle 60
The flying trapeze act required split-second precision to avoid an accident. The cue was provided by the band conducted by Arthur playing the "Minute Waltz" by Chopin and the trapeze exchange was to take place at the last note precisely. All Arthur had to do was to speed up the music by a mere one or two seconds.

Puzzle 61

Puzzle 62

8	2	4	5	9	3	1	7	6
6	9	1	7	2	4	5	8	3
5	7	3	1	8	6	4	9	2
1	5	7	2	6	9	3	4	8
4	6	2	3	1	8	7	5	9
3	8	9	4	7	5	6	2	1
9	3	8	6	5	7	2	1	4
7	1	6	9	4	2	8	3	5
2	4	5	8	3	1	9	6	7

Puzzle 63
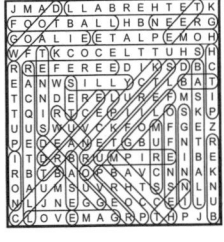

Puzzle 65

Puzzle 66

2	6	4	3	1	7	8	5	9
5	1	9	6	4	8	7	2	3
3	7	8	2	5	9	4	1	6
4	2	1	5	3	6	9	7	8
9	8	3	1	7	4	2	6	5
6	5	7	9	8	2	1	3	4
8	9	6	7	2	3	5	4	1
7	3	5	4	9	1	6	8	2
1	4	2	8	6	5	3	9	7

Puzzle 67
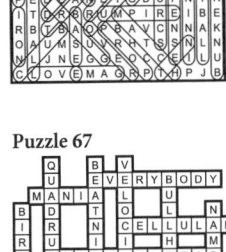

Puzzle 68

Puzzle 70
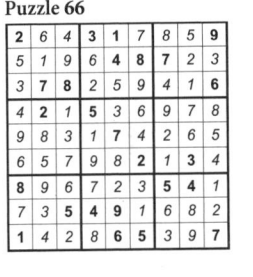

Puzzle 71

5	1	8	4	3	9	6	2	7
9	7	6	1	5	2	4	3	8
2	4	3	6	8	7	9	5	1
7	2	4	8	9	6	3	1	5
6	5	9	7	1	3	8	4	2
3	8	1	2	4	5	7	6	9
8	6	2	3	7	1	5	9	4
1	9	7	5	6	4	2	8	3
4	3	5	9	2	8	1	7	6

Answers

Puzzle 72

Hans was an undercover agent for the special anti-terrorist unit and had succeeded in infiltrating the cell. When the official was kidnapped and sentenced, Helldorf volunteered to perform the execution in order to save the man's life. He shot him with blanks; the blood was a "special effects" exercise with the props supplied by Hans. The press was misled by the police to avoid blowing Helldorf's cover.

Puzzle 73

A crossword grid with answers including: HALO, CRATER, DACE, EARWIG, BANE, SUET, DRUDGE, LUSH, AWE, SAUCER, SLAM.

Puzzle 74

A crossword grid with answers including: COUNCIL HOUSE, KUNG FU, TOWERING, INEXPERIENCE, INADVERTENT, BOSUN, RERUN, YEARN, BUSINESSMAN.

Puzzle 75

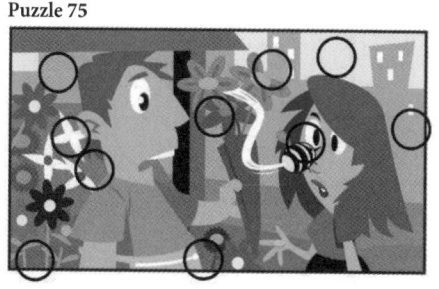

Puzzle 76

A crossword grid with answers including: SAGE, SWOT, APARTMENT, DESIGN, SCOT, TRUE, BRASSY, IMPASSIVE, PAGE, TREK.

Puzzle 77

7	5	1	6	3	2	4	9	8
4	2	9	1	7	8	3	6	5
8	3	6	4	9	5	7	2	1
2	6	3	5	8	4	1	7	9
5	1	7	2	6	9	8	4	3
9	4	8	7	1	3	2	5	6
1	9	2	8	4	6	5	3	7
3	7	5	9	2	1	6	8	4
6	8	4	3	5	7	9	1	2

Puzzle 78

Tom took one of his sausages and held it out of reach but within Kim's smelling distance. He began circling the tree with the dog following greedily until, after several revolutions, the leash winding around the tree became short enough, enabling Tom to retrieve his hat.

Puzzle 79

Puzzle 80

A word search grid containing hidden words including: TUNGSTEN, HAFNIUM.

Answers

Puzzle 81

Puzzle 82

2 1 3 0 3 0 1 2

Puzzle 83

Puzzle 84

Puzzle 85

Puzzle 86

Puzzle 87

Puzzle 88

2 1 1 2 1 1

Puzzle 89

Puzzle 91

Puzzle 92

Puzzle 93
Answer: 3.
Multiply the opposite corners and subtract the lower total from the higher one.
9 × 2 = 18.
5 × 3 = 15.
18 − 15 = 3

Answers

Puzzle 94

4	9	3	1	5	6	7	2	8
5	2	1	8	7	9	6	4	3
6	8	7	3	2	4	1	9	5
2	4	9	5	6	8	3	7	1
7	1	5	9	3	2	4	8	6
3	6	8	4	1	7	9	5	2
8	5	6	7	9	1	2	3	4
9	3	2	6	4	5	8	1	7
1	7	4	2	8	3	5	6	9

Puzzle 95

Puzzle 96

Puzzle 97
The soldier had been dreaming while he was in fact supposed to be on guard duty.

Puzzle 99
Ronnie Breskal is a film star and Ernesto Saler his stand-in stuntman. They were filming a scene for their latest adventure movie.

Puzzle 98

Puzzle 100
Each time Philip bets 500 francs on red, Deborah places 500 francs on black. Because of zero, they lose their stake about once in every 74 throws, but Deborah accepts this modest loss. The activity keeps her husband happy and they both enjoy the exciting ambiance of the casino.

Puzzle 102

Answers

Puzzle 103

5	8	9	6	1	7	4	3	2
4	3	7	8	2	9	5	1	6
6	1	2	3	4	5	7	8	9
1	9	5	4	8	3	6	2	7
2	7	4	9	6	1	8	5	3
8	6	3	7	5	2	9	4	1
7	2	8	5	3	6	1	9	4
9	4	1	2	7	8	3	6	5
3	5	6	1	9	4	2	7	8

Puzzle 104

Puzzle 105

John is 1 year old.

Puzzle 106

Puzzle 107

Puzzle 108

Puzzle 109

6	1	3	2	9	4	5	8	7
5	4	9	7	8	1	3	6	2
8	2	7	6	3	5	9	4	1
2	8	6	1	7	9	4	3	5
3	5	1	4	2	8	7	9	6
7	9	4	5	6	3	1	2	8
9	3	2	8	5	7	6	1	4
1	7	8	9	4	6	2	5	3
4	6	5	3	1	2	8	7	9

Puzzle 110

Puzzle 111

Puzzle 112

Dr Bernstein had an enlargement done of the photograph and managed to decipher the address of the recipient of the newspaper which had been written by the newsagent in the top corner of the front page.

Answers

Puzzle 113

Puzzle 114

9	5	4	3	8	7	1	2	6
7	6	8	2	1	9	5	4	3
3	1	2	6	4	5	7	9	8
6	2	5	9	3	1	4	8	7
1	7	3	8	6	4	9	5	2
4	8	9	5	7	2	6	3	1
5	9	6	1	2	8	3	7	4
8	3	7	4	9	6	2	1	5
2	4	1	7	5	3	8	6	9

Puzzle 115

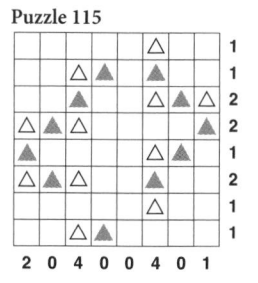

Puzzle 116

Puzzle 117

The date was the 1st of April, and Martin was the victim of a practical joke. His colleagues in the mail room had Martin's invitation specially printed, referring to a fancy-dress party, while all others specified "formal dress."

Puzzle 118

Puzzle 119

Puzzle 120

3	1		2		2
	2	2	2	2	2
2	1		3	3	
2	1	2	2	2	2
	2		2		1
3	1	2	3	1	0

Puzzle 121

Faced with Mario's reluctance, the boss of all bosses hired a contract killer, who had shot Sylvia several hours before Mario's bullet. A post-mortem found that it was the first shot that killed Sylvia. When Mario entered the apartment, Sylvia was not asleep, but dead. As there is no law against shooting a corpse, Mario had to be released.

Puzzle 122

D and I are the pair.

Answers

Puzzle 123

Puzzle 124

Puzzle 125

Puzzle 126

2	7	4	1	8	9	6	5	3
8	1	3	7	5	6	4	2	9
5	6	9	4	3	2	8	7	1
3	5	8	6	4	7	1	9	2
9	2	6	8	1	3	7	4	5
1	4	7	9	2	5	3	8	6
7	3	1	2	9	8	5	6	4
6	9	5	3	7	4	2	1	8
4	8	2	5	6	1	9	3	7

Puzzle 127

G.

Puzzle 128

Puzzle 129

This is a true story. A chain of bookmakers opening a new shop issued a tender for a telephone and loudspeaker system. Ollie's customer quoted low and won, installing Ollie's gadget. This had the effect that the running commentary of the race was received in the shop five minutes after the start. Punters belonging to the ring could listen to the broadcast through a portable radio and still place a bet when the race was sufficiently advanced, or indeed over, to identify the winning horse. This scam was used in the movie The Sting although there the scam was operated manually.

Puzzle 130

3	7	9	5	4	6	8	2	1
2	1	5	3	9	8	4	6	7
6	4	8	7	2	1	9	3	5
1	9	6	4	8	2	7	5	3
5	3	2	6	7	9	1	8	4
4	8	7	1	5	3	6	9	2
7	6	1	8	3	5	2	4	9
9	5	4	2	6	7	3	1	8
8	2	3	9	1	4	5	7	6

Puzzle 131

Answer: 16. Subtract the smallest corner number from the largest, then subtract the smaller of the two remaining corners from the larger, then multiply the two totals.

9 – 1 = 8, 8 – 6 = 2. 8 x 2 = 16

Puzzle 132

B and F are the pair.

Puzzle 133

Answers

Puzzle 134

The restaurant owner had a slot machine installed on his premises by a criminal gang. A rival mob had forced him to install one of their machines, with guaranteed protection. When the original gang heard of the second machine they sent one of their heavies along to smash it up. After he left, the restaurant owner called the mob and told them what had happened, whereupon they eliminated the heavy.

Puzzle 135

1	7	3	2	4	8	6	5	9
5	8	9	6	3	7	2	4	1
6	2	4	1	5	9	8	3	7
4	5	1	7	8	2	3	9	6
2	6	7	5	9	3	4	1	8
9	3	8	4	6	1	5	7	2
8	4	5	9	7	6	1	2	3
3	9	2	8	1	5	7	6	4
7	1	6	3	2	4	9	8	5

Puzzle 136

The border between Turkey and Iraq runs across the mountain, with the peak being on the Iraqi side.

Puzzle 137

Puzzle 138

Jaime had instantly realized, when Moses turned purple, that he was choking. He had first struck him on the back to try and dislodge the offending piece of food. When that failed, he had performed an emergency tracheotomy (opening the trachea, or windpipe, to provide a means of breathing when the natural air passage is obstructed above this level), thereby saving Moses' life.

Puzzle 139

Peter Collins was in fact a policeman. The trial had been a set-up to enable him to gain the confidence of the Mafia contract killer and obtain evidence for a forthcoming Senate investigation.

Puzzle 140

Bobby was a Labrador and John, his master, had used a dog whistle, inaudible to the human ear, to call him.

Puzzle 141

Because of the sudden illness of the leading actor, the French farce was replaced with a stand-by performance of Hamlet. The manager had failed to inform his crew of the programme change.

Puzzle 142

Answers

Puzzle 143

S	L	Y	L	Y		W	A	F	E	R
	E		I			R		X		
F	A	C	E		K	I	T	B	A	G
	S		G		A			L		
R	E	V	E	A	L		M	O	T	H
			L							
G	L	E	N		I	N	S	I	S	T
	L				S		I		P	
R	A	B	B	E	T		S	N	A	P
	M		Y		I		A		W	
M	A	N	E	S		C	L	I	N	K

Puzzle 144

This is essentially a true story, except for chronological inaccuracy. During 1970, one Udo Proksch of Vienna founded an association promoting the idea that corpses should be buried in a vertical position. The project attracted many prominent proponents from all sections of Austrian society. In later years Proksch became notorious in connection with an insurance fraud which cost the life of six men. Udo Proksch was sentenced to life imprisonment and died in prison.

Puzzle 145

8	5	7	4	6	2	3	9	1
2	1	4	3	7	9	8	5	6
3	9	6	5	8	1	7	4	2
1	6	8	7	2	4	9	3	5
4	2	5	9	1	3	6	7	8
7	3	9	6	5	8	2	1	4
6	4	3	8	9	5	1	2	7
9	7	1	2	4	6	5	8	3
5	8	2	1	3	7	4	6	9

Puzzle 146

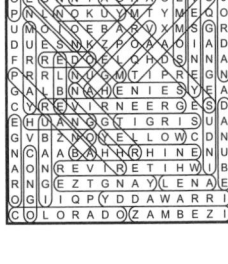

Puzzle 147

8	7	6	9	2	3	4	1	5
1	2	4	8	7	5	3	9	6
9	5	3	1	6	4	7	2	8
7	3	1	2	4	8	6	5	9
4	8	9	3	5	6	2	7	1
5	6	2	7	1	9	8	3	4
2	1	5	4	8	7	9	6	3
6	9	8	5	3	2	1	4	7
3	4	7	6	9	1	5	8	2

Puzzle 148

Puzzle 149

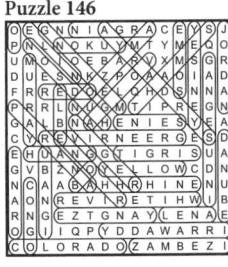

Puzzle 150

Puzzle 151

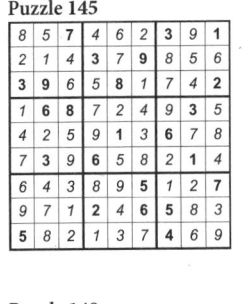

Puzzle 152

Tessino was shot in a drive-in cinema during a war scene.

Puzzle 153

M		B					E		S
A	P	R	O	P	O	S		D	N	A
R		E		R		P		G		V
S	H	A	L	E		O	X	E	Y	E
H		S		V		R				
Y	E	T		A	N	T		H	O	B
				L			S		E	A
P	A	S	T	E		C	A	R	E	R
E		L		N		A		B		R
A	D	O		T	E	R	R	A	C	E
L		W						L		N

Answers

Puzzle 154

S	H	E	B	A	N	G		M	O	T	I	F

THENCEFORWARD grid answers include: SHEBANG, MOTIF, THENCEFORWARD, NAG, HEADPIECE, BUNDLE, FRENZY, DAYSCHOOL, OUR, VEXEDQUESTION, LETUP, DESKTOP.

Cipher: R S Z A Q X V B H F K E / N T U D Y O M J P G W L C

Puzzle 155

Wordsearch grid.

Puzzle 156

The items are timepieces. A grandfather clock would be too heavy to carry. An hourglass has many thousands of grains of sand. A mechanical clock has eight to ten moving parts. A sundial has no moving parts.

Puzzle 157

3	8	7	2	9	5	6	4	1
4	9	6	8	1	7	2	5	3
5	1	2	3	4	6	7	8	9
8	7	4	6	3	2	9	1	5
1	6	5	9	8	4	3	2	7
2	3	9	7	5	1	8	6	4
6	4	8	1	7	9	5	3	2
7	5	3	4	2	8	1	9	6
9	2	1	5	6	3	4	7	8

Puzzle 158

Crossword grid answers include: BRAVURA, SASH, CANINE, SATE, DOSE, SUSS, BLAH, YANKEE, SQUEEZE, YALE.

Puzzle 159

Number grid puzzle.

Puzzle 160

UNSAVED, CUFFS grid answers include: UNSAVED, CUFFS, BOXCLEVER, LARVA, SOMEHOW, BILLET, GAZUMP, LIQUEFY, JABOT, ONIONSKIN, VIA, RHYME, TETANUS.

Cipher: A W E Y V L S C K O T J Z / F G I P Q M X U B D R N H

Puzzle 161

Crossword grid answers include: ISSUE, WAGER, NAME, ABROAD, CONCRETE, ARTISTIC, VALISE, SEAM, LEVER, GAVEL.

192